100

THINGS TO DO IN
SANTA FE
BEFORE YOU
DIE

100
THINGS TO DO IN
SANTA FE
BEFORE YOU
DIE

JEFF BERG

Library of Congress Control Number: 2019936721

ISBN: 9781681062310

Design by Jill Halpin

Photos by Ysabel Velarde

Printed in the United States of America
19 20 21 22 23   5 4 3 2 1

Please note that websites, phone numbers, addresses, and company names are subject to change or cancellation. We did our best to relay the most accurate information available, but due to circumstances beyond our control, please do not hold us liable for misinformation. When exploring new destinations, please do your homework before you go.

DEDICATION

Dedicated to everyone who works at an animal shelter.
Thanks for making a difference!

CONTENTS

Preface. xiii

Acknowledgments. xv

Food and Drink

1. Put on Your Bib at Harry's Roadhouse 2
2. Eat, Drink, Sing at Cowgirl BBQ 3
3. Experience Africa at the Jambo Café. 4
4. Do Your Body Good at Sweetwater Harvest Kitchen 5
5. Relax and Eat Well at Love Yourself Café. 6
6. Give a Hoot at Sabor Peruano 7
7. Pass by Mickey D's for Bumble Bee's Baja Grill 8
8. Practice Your French at L'Olivier 9
9. Brake for Food Trucks Here, There, and Everywhere! 10
10. Wine and Dine at Il Piatto Italian Farmhouse Kitchen 12
11. Tune Up Your Carb-O-Rater at This Homestyle Café 13
12. Check Out What's Cookin' in the Pantry. 14
13. Go to Rio and Points South Via La Plancha de Eldorado 15
14. Could Café Fina Be New Mexico's Last Chance Gulch? 16
15. Looking for Local with a Twist? Try Tia Sophia's 17
16. Show Off Your Good Taste: Geronimo 18
17. Meet and Greet Southwestern Style at Mucho Gusto 20
18. Experience the Paper(thin) Dosas of Indian Cuisine 22

• •

19. Savor a Touch of the Grape 23

20. Have a Barley Sandwich! 24

21. Watch for Celebrities from Your Perch at the Teahouse 26

22. Not Just Another Tequila Sunrise at the Santa Fe Margarita Trail . 28

Music and Entertainment

23. Appreciate Real Cinema 32

24. And Speaking of Movies . . . Attend Not One But Two
Film Festivals 34

25. Make Film History in Santa Fe! 35

26. Picture Yourself on the Set of a Western at Eaves and Bonanza . . . 36

27. Catch the Last Picture Show 38

28. Immerse Yourself in Musica 39

29. Celebrate Mystical Art 40

30. Discover the Crawling, the Flying, and the Creeping at Harrell
House Bug Museum 41

31. Shut Up and Play All the Hits! 42

32. Showcasing Art in Public Places 43

33. Speaking of Art . . . Seek Out the Santa Fe Gallery Association . . 44

34. Give Opera a Chance 45

35. Be Entertained by New Mexico Politics 46

36. Meditate on the Haiku Pathway 47

37. Feelin' Lucky? 48

38. Learn to Read the Stars 49

● ●

Sports and Recreation

39. Ski Rugged Mountain Terrain 52

40. Break Out the Peanuts and Cracker Jacks 53

41. Float through Life on a Raft! 54

42. Hike the Dale Ball Trails 56

43. Explore New Mexico Terrain. 57

44. Get Your Outdoor Self On at Hyde Memorial State Park 58

45. Wander New Mexico 60

46. Tour Santa Fe on Two Wheels. 61

47. Go Soak Your Head in a Hot Spring Pool 63

48. Visit the Historic Walks of Santa Fe 64

49. Have an Authentic Western Adventure on Horseback. 65

Culture and History

50. Make a Wish When You Enter This Place of Worship 68

51. Schedule Your Dream Wedding at the Loretto Chapel 69

52. Visit the Site of Japanese Internment. 70

53. Be a Temporary Local in the Plaza (Not Playa). 71

54. Be Seen, but Not Heard at the Sante Fe Children's Museum 72

55. Indulge in Hot Wax Art at the Museum of Encaustic Art 74

56. Tour (One of) the Oldest Houses in the United States (?) 75

57. Travel the Old El Camino Real Santa Fe 76

58. Get Your Kicks on Route 66 77

59. Is It True about the Other Aliens? 78

60. Look for Fact, not Fiction at the New Mexico Military Museum . . 80

• •

61. Pick Up a Second House: Cerro Pelon Ranch 81

62. Add to Your Life List at the Randall Davey Audubon Center and Sanctuary. 82

63. Study New Mexico History in a New Museum 83

64. Watch the Sunset from Cross of the Martyrs Park. 84

65. Dance It Up at El Rancho de las Golondrinas 86

66. Peruse Artifacts of Indian Arts and Culture. 88

67. Marvel at the Skill of Native American Jewelers at the Wheelwright. 89

68. Prepare to Be Awed by Spanish Colonial Folk Art 90

69. Delve into International Folk Art. 91

70. While You're in the Neighborhood . . . Visit the Santa Fe Botanical Garden 92

71. Walk among the Best of Contemporary Native Arts 94

72. Something for Everyone at El Museo Cultural de Santa Fe 95

73. Focus on International Art at the Ralph T. Coe Center 96

74. Celebrate a New Mexico Art Icon 97

75. Cleanse Your Bad Juju at the Burning of Zozobra 98

76. Shop and Socialize at Ye Olde Indian Market 99

77. Try Unusual Pairings at the Wine and Chile Fiesta. 100

78. Test Your Stamina at the Green Chile Cheeseburger Smackdown . . 101

79. Sponsor a New Artist at the Spanish Market 102

80. Sip n' Slurp at the Souper Bowl. 103

81. Salute One More Ephemeral Event 104

82. Show Some LGBTQ Pride. 105

83. Ditch the Car!. 106

• •

84. Weather or Not 108

85. Day Trippin' at Valles Caldera and Jemez Springs 110

86. Discover Little-Known New Mexico History at Pecos Park 111

87. No Sleeping in These Tents! 112

88. Climb into Cliff Dwellings at Bandelier 113

89. View Iconic Petroglyphs in La Cienequilla 114

90. Cruise the Back Road to Madrid 115

Shopping and Fashion

91. "A Place Is Not Really a Place without a Bookstore" 118

92. Find a New Family Member 120

93. Keep that Christmas Spirit Going 122

94. Say Hey, Dood at Doodlet's 124

95. Get Cosmic, Man! 126

96. Celebrate Old School at Red River Mercantile 127

97. Shop with Confidence at Harry's Clothing 128

98. Find Earth-Friendly Goods at Maya Santa Fe 130

99. Believe It: "And All Your Future Lies beneath Your Hat" 132

100. Escape the Burning Rays in a Montecristi Custom Hat 133

Suggested Itineraries 135

Activities by Season 138

Index 140

• •

PREFACE

For years and years I wanted to move to New Mexico. Somehow, when visiting, it got a hook into me that never let go. Hence, I am glad I am here, and I wanted to share a bit of what I've discovered while living in Santa Fe. Get busy!

· ·

ACKNOWLEDGMENTS

Many thanks to Ysabel Velarde, who did all the photographs for the book, and to author Max Evans, who really put a burr under my saddle that helped me become a highly motivated writer.

FOOD AND DRINK

PUT ON YOUR BIB
AT HARRY'S ROADHOUSE

For a city of eighty-five thousand, Santa Fe has—are you ready?— nearly two hundred restaurants. Admittedly, tourism is one of the city's biggest revenue draws, but even the locals seem to like to dine out.

Most ethnic cuisines are covered, from Caribbean-African to Peruvian. About the only things missing in Santa Fe are a sit-down Greek café and Ethiopian fare. Vegans and vegetarians are well served by a number of bistros and cafés.

And of course there are numerous food trucks and more than ninety restaurants that serve some variation of the native New Mexican/Mexican cuisine.

My choice for the best of the best? Harry's Roadhouse. I'm a vegetarian leaning vegan, and it covers the gamut. It has a full bar, the best patio in the area, and a great list of daily specials.

96 B Old Las Vegas Hwy., 505-989-4629
harrysroadhousesantafe.com

EAT, DRINK, SING
AT COWGIRL BBQ

Besides having a great and varied menu and being a supporter of many community activities, the Cowgirl is certainly the most unique "theme" restaurant in the city, honoring—guess who?—cowgirls!

It has a funky bar, wooden floors, servers who wear cowboy hats and jeans, and a menu that offers something for everyone, from vegetarian (try the butternut squash casserole . . . oh, my!) to BBQ, along with music, dancing, a next-door pool hall, and the second-best patio for dining in the city (trailing Harry's Roadhouse).

The Cowgirl also hosts Monday night Cowgirl Karaoke and live music every night of the week. This joint is open daily, as is the New York West Village version in case you happen to be in that 'hood.

319 S. Guadalupe, 505-982-2565
cowgirlsantafe.com

EXPERIENCE AFRICA
AT THE JAMBO CAFÉ

The African cuisine in this restaurant is truly amazing. Owned by chef Ahmed Obo, the location in a nondescript strip mall is well worth finding.

Obo often wins cooking contests, and the restaurant has been featured on the Food Network's *Diners, Drive-ins, and Dives*. Since opening in 2009, it has become a favorite of the locals and has added a food truck called Jambo Hapa (meaning "here" in Swahili) and Jambo Imports, a store with authentic African goods, spices, and foods. A portion of each sale goes to the Jambo Kids Foundation.

The menu here is as varied as can be, ranging from coconut shrimp to a delicious savory stuffed phyllo.

2010 Cerrillos Rd., 505-473-1269
jambocafe.net

DO YOUR BODY GOOD
AT SWEETWATER HARVEST KITCHEN

A slightly out-of-the-way place, Sweetwater Harvest Kitchen has a wide-ranging menu and is perhaps one of the more environmentally friendly eateries in town, actively composting, recycling, and sourcing properly. SHK donates to local charities, such as the Santa Fe Children's Museum, and it also serves some of the best food in town, which includes accommodating those with alternative lifestyles by offering vegan versions of many of its dishes.

Breakfast can include buckwheat banana pancakes. Lunch offers tricolor quinoa cakes, while dinner can get you a wonderful order of warm glass noodle soup, featuring yam noodles, veggies, and your choice of protein, ranging from buffalo sausage to tempeh.

As a bonus, it has an outstanding Sunday brunch, offering paleo burritos and pumpkin pancakes. Sweetwater also serves wine, beer, and gluten-free desserts.

1512-B Pacheco, 505-795-7383
sweetwatersf.com

RELAX AND EAT WELL
AT LOVE YOURSELF CAFÉ

Although it sounds like it might be for folks who appreciate Yanni and crystals, this unique café is all that and more.

It has one of the warmest and most welcoming atmospheres of any restaurant in Santa Fe and offers many seasonal and farm-to-table meals. It specializes in herbal elixirs and offers mostly vegan plates, but even carnivores can find themselves something delicious here.

The restaurant presents everything from white pizzas to Guatemalan potato cakes, so you can't help but feel healthier after dining here.

In addition, it is attached to the Light Vessel spa, which is a full-service wellness salon offering custom massages and facials and lesser-known treatments such as Thai foot reflexology and a cryosauna, a type of cold-temperature therapy that is thought to help reduce inflammation, reduce muscle soreness, and promote better sleep.

199-D Paseo de Peralta (east end of De Vargas Mall)
505-983-5683 or 505-473-1200
lightvesselsantafe.com

GIVE A HOOT
AT SABOR PERUANO

I suspect that Santa Fe is the smallest city in the known universe to have a Peruvian restaurant, that being Sabor Peruano (translating loosely to "taste of Peru"), housed in the middle of a now-thriving shopping mall.

Sabor Peruano offers traditional Peruvian dishes, such as *aji de gallina*, a chicken breast in a mild yellow pepper sauce, served with sides of golden potatoes, olives, and a hard-boiled egg, all topped with Parmesan cheese. Much to my surprise, the restaurant offers an extensive vegan menu, which includes *papa rellena*, a featherlight mix of mashed potatoes, olives, onions, raisins, mushrooms, and spices, which is somehow deep fried.

The café also has a "side order" of Peruvian goods, from small home decorations to beautiful and traditional clothing.

Sabor Peruano is operated by two sisters who are, guess what, originally from Peru. The service and offerings are amazing and make for an interesting cultural adventure.

My first girlfriend spent a semester in Peru. She never wrote me. I was sad but stupid because I loved her anyway.

163 Paseo de Peralta (inside DeVargas Mall)
505-358-3529
saborperuanosf.com

PASS BY MICKEY D'S
FOR BUMBLE BEE'S BAJA GRILL

In a town that has dozens of Mexican restaurants (even Chipotle is opening soon), Bumble Bee's Baja Grill makes good, fresh food faster and cheaper than most other places.

Its concept is simple—first, provide an extensive menu that is vegetarian and vegan friendly, then have customers order at the counter, get a number, and find a place to sit. In just a few minutes, servers arrive with some of the best food in the city, often at a reasonable price (a bean and rice bowl costs about $5).

Even though the service is minimal, it is great because of experienced staff who have been on hand for years, an anomaly in Santa Fe, home of high staff turnover in its many restaurants.

The restaurant started after owner "Bumble Bee Bob"—who drives a yellow and black Mini Cooper—went to Mexico and was impressed with the culture, food, and people and decided to try his hand at fresh (yes), fast (yes), and casual (yes) Mexican-style food at a fair price.

BBB now lives in Mexico part time with BJ, his wife, but any residuals he still receives from the amazing burritos and salmon plates are well deserved.

301 Jefferson, 505-820-2862
bumblebeesbajagrill.com

PRACTICE YOUR FRENCH
AT L'OLIVIER

Countless other restaurants have operated out of this space over the years, but L'Olivier, a casual and intimate French café, seems to have found the secret.

Possibly the only restaurant in Santa Fe that offers "only" French-style food, L'Olivier bases its success on attentive service and a pretty generous menu.

The restaurant is operated by Parisian chef Xavier Grenet, who has worked at fine restaurants in New York and San Francisco, and Nathalie Bonnard-Grenet, who is also a native Parisian and a Level One sommelier.

It is located just off the plaza, and it uses as many local ingredients as possible while growing its own extensive array of herbs. Other items that it purchases locally when possible include kale, squash blossoms, goat cheese, garlic, apples, and cherry tomatoes.

Of course, there is an extensive wine list, holiday specials, and a unique prix fixe dinner on Tuesday and Wednesday.

What to try? My dining companion swears by the fish of the day, and I like the roasted squash or the veggie risotto when available.

229 Galisteo, 505-989-1919
loliviersantafe.com

BRAKE FOR FOOD TRUCKS
HERE, THERE, AND EVERYWHERE!

Food trucks are big everywhere nowadays. I wouldn't be surprised to see a food truck "mall" somewhere, sometime soon.

Santa Fe is no exception, although please note that some of the trucks listed below may be gone by the time you read this. If so, there are probably any number to replace them.

Here are some of the better, and often more popular, stops for you to consider. Caveat emptor: the addresses shown were accurate at press time! Also beware of changes in operating hours.

Bang Bite Filling Station: Operating since 2013, this place is one of the more established and perhaps least likely-to-move trucks in Santa Fe. The menu varies from day to day and targets hearty carnivores. It receives consistently good reviews on social media. The Bang Burger features bacon, asadero cheese, green chile, a fried egg, and green chile aioli. Lordy!

2791 Agua Fria

Bonsai Asian Tacos: Certainly offering one of the more unique truck menus, Bonsai crosses Korean and sometimes other Asian foods with a Mexican bill o' fare to create its own unique offerings. You can find salmon tempura tacos on the menu next to pomegranate duck tacos or tacos made with pulled pork.

1599 St. Francis Dr., 505-316-9418

El Sabor: This old-time truck has a great location and seems to be constantly busy when the New Mexico legislature, located across the street, is in session. The tempting aromas of shrimp or fish tacos, agua fresca (a quenching and sweet Mexican soft drink), sautéed spinach tapas, and a crispy avocado sandwich from the truck menu permeate the area, with the place getting consistently good reviews.

518 Old Santa Fe Trail, 505-316-5084

Root 66: located near the popular coffee spot, Iconik Coffee, Root 66 suits my tastes perfectly because it is a rarity: a truck that has a complete vegan menu.

Root 66's menu offers the impossibly delicious Impossible Burger, a new vegan delight that even the most carnivorous carnivore would be tempted to try. It also has excellent fries, meat-free gumbo, and even "crab"-cake sandwiches. Please note that sometimes Root 66 closes in the winter, but if you are inclined to give something new a try, here is your chance. If you are looking for ambience (and a brew to pair with your Impossible), you can take your meal into the beer parlor to dine as well.

1704 Lena St.

It's Greek to Me: As I mentioned before, one of the few types of food that is sorely lacking in Santa Fe is a sit-down Greek restaurant. However, with the recent addition of this food truck, operated by chef Kerry Tramontanas, that wait might not seem so long.

Tramontanas's menu is varied and interesting, offering traditional Greek dishes such as souvlaki and gyros, along with a gyro burger or patty melt. There are also fried Greek-style potatoes that will make you wonder why you ever ordered the other kind.

502 Old Santa Fe Trail, 505-699-5651

WINE AND DINE
AT IL PIATTO ITALIAN FARMHOUSE KITCHEN

Another well-established and relaxing café is Il Piatto, which has been around for more than twenty years. It expanded in recent years but kept the charm and casual atmosphere that makes this Italian place a continuous draw, because you don't have to wear starched white collars or floor-length dresses to eat here.

As is the trend among restaurants that care nowadays, Il Piatto does its best to use supplies from local farms, including wheat flour from a local miller, meat from local livestock suppliers, and organic vegetables from the Green Tractor Farm down the road. It also uses products from the Santa Fe Farmers' Market as much as possible.

It all works quite well, and it has become famous in the area for such things as the pumpkin ravioli and the walnut-gorgonzola ravioli.

Wine Spectator has taken note of Il Piatto's amazing wine list, recognizing it with the Wine Excellence award for the last four years.

95 W. Marcy St., 505-984-1091
ilpiattosantafe.com

TUNE UP YOUR CARB-O-RATER
AT THIS HOMESTYLE CAFÉ

Another casual and unique place (in case you haven't noticed, I've mostly avoided the expensive and/or pretentious), this curious little diner is hidden away in a residential area rather by itself.

Its precursor was a place called "Dave's Not Here," perhaps a take on the famous Cheech and Chong bit where Dave "wasn't" there, but this place retains the atmosphere and great menu of its stepparent. The Tune-up Café, along with several other out-of-the-way places, was featured on *Diners, Drive-Ins, and Dives.*

The Tune-up has a small bar and an array of oddball tables, and you order at the counter. The menu includes breakfast, weekend brunch, lunch, and dinner.

Among its offerings are banana leaf-wrapped tamales, Cubano sandwiches, El Salvadoran pupusas, and a sizable breakfast burrito.

As for Dave, no one knows for sure where he is nowadays, but some believe that's him in the back booth, feasting on the huevos rancheros.

1115 Hickox St., 505-983-7060
tuneupsantafe.com

CHECK OUT WHAT'S COOKIN'
IN THE PANTRY

Perhaps Santa Fe's oldest continuously operating restaurant, the Pantry, a small place that is well loved by locals, almost always has a line waiting at the busiest hours—often weekend breakfast.

Starting in 1948, the place has been offering good old-fashioned comfort food, which it does with pizzazz, flavor (the food is made mostly from scratch), and affordability. In 2018 the café received an Award of Excellence from Trip Advisor.

The website notes that it serves "three-hundred thousand eggs a year, twenty-six tons of potatoes, seven tons of—you guessed it—green chile, and two tons of coffee." With that kind of volume, you know the Pantry is a local hot spot.

Advertising itself as "Santa Fe's Meeting Place," the Pantry is the place to rendezvous with some friends for huevos consuelo or the patty melt. You're welcome!

1820 Cerrillos Rd., 505-986-0022
pantrysantafe.com

GO TO RIO AND POINTS SOUTH
VIA LA PLANCHA DE ELDORADO

Often overlooked because of its out-of-the-way location (ten miles out in the El Dorado subdivision), La Plancha, which specializes in South American cuisine, is a homey place with a full bar and often has live music that fits the atmosphere.

Part of Santa Fe, the El Dorado area has about 2,500 residents in a housing development that is somewhat self-sufficient and very quiet. It is also where I hide out.

La Plancha is owned by chef Juan Carlos Pineda and his family. Pineda has over twenty-five years of experience and the menu offers a few popular fusion-style treats that have helped La Plancha (the Griddle) stay open for ten years. It also offers a Sunday brunch.

La Plancha is the only place in Santa Fe that I know of that makes a loroco omelet, which includes the flowers of the loroco plant, spinach, scallions, mushrooms, tomatoes, and cheese—and is also one of two places that offer green rice as a side for several dishes. Sorry, no green eggs or ham. Also known for the New Mexico fettuccine and Salvadoran tamales, La Plancha is well worth the short drive.

7 Caliente Rd., 505-466-2060
laplanchadeeldorado.com

COULD CAFÉ FINA
BE NEW MEXICO'S
LAST CHANCE GULCH?

Housed in a converted gas station, Café Fina is another favorite of locals, and rightfully so. It is open for a sort-of brunch from 7 a.m. to 3 p.m. daily and for dinner from Thursday through Saturday. Like La Plancha, it is about ten miles out of town, just off I-25 as you head north, and it is probably the last great restaurant in the state as one heads toward Colorado. Sorry, residents of Pecos, Las Vegas, and Raton . . . I tried!

It is also community oriented and somewhat vegetarian friendly, with a pleasant beer and wine menu. Cloud cakes are made with ricotta and served with berries; *huevos motulenos*, a personal favorite, consists of two eggs on a tortilla covered with feta cheese, peas, black beans, and sautéed banana.

Dinner offerings include Vietnamese shrimp, served with mung bean noodles, cabbage, peanuts, and sweet herbs. Or perhaps you are more in the mood for vegetarian or chicken enchiladas— gently smothered with chile (not chili) and cheese.

624 Old Las Vegas Hwy., 505-466-3886
cafefinasantafe.com

LOOKING FOR LOCAL WITH A TWIST?
TRY TIA SOPHIA'S

I'd be remiss if I didn't offer more choices for local food or variations thereof, and Tia Sophia's is one of the best. It is a simple but welcoming place that serves only breakfast and lunch, is open daily, and is just a tiny distance from the plaza, across from the stately Lensic Theater.

If you are lucky, Carl will still be working there, and he will be your server. If so, be prepared for some of the most eye-rolling jokes ever. The whole atmosphere is casual and fun, and because—at least to me—"local food" can sometimes mean "no variety," Tia Sophia's will quickly disabuse you of that notion.

Its breakfast burritos are a local legend and have been served in this diner-type restaurant and shotgun-style building since 1975. There are daily breakfast specials, and the menu is simple but enticing. It is mostly New Mexican/Mexican fare, but the lunch menu also includes some sandwiches and salads. However, you should opt for the Santa Fe Plate. With most orders, you also get a sopaipilla, which is like a pillowy deep-fried cloud that you dip in honey.

210 W. San Francisco, 505-983-9880
tiasophias.com

SHOW OFF YOUR GOOD TASTE:
GERONIMO

Geronimo is one of the better-known and snazzier places in Santa Fe and wears its reputation well.

Located in the circa-1756 "Borrego house" which was built by Geronimo Lopez, this cozy adobe structure is truly inviting, and during the cooler months warmth from the working kiva fireplaces increases the ambience four-square. Geronimo has received so many awards that I can't even list them here, they are all prestigious and include four diamonds from AAA and four stars from *Forbes*.

The chef is Sllin Cruz, who took over several years ago after the untimely death of Eric DiStefano, who helped make Geronimo Geronimo.

The menu? Funny you should ask. How about starting with a Fujisaki pear salad, which includes Bleu d'Auvergne "grilled" cheese, watercress, cashews, and arugula. Follow that with cast-iron seared diver scallops, which come with asparagus, sweet corn, Israeli couscous, and a beurre blanc sauce, and then finish up with tropical coconut sorbet.

724 Canyon Rd., 505-982-1500
geronimorestaurant.com

TIP

Geronimo is vegetarian/vegan friendly, has a fully stocked lounge, and is open only for dinner. But oh, what a dinner!

MEET AND GREET SOUTHWESTERN STYLE
AT MUCHO GUSTO

Want to know a secret? Sidle on over here, and I'll tell you one.

Skip all those beaneries that cater to tourists and look like haciendas or rancheros. Fly by those that offer "gringo"-style Mexican food. And don't you dare go near Taco Bell for a meal that can easily be beat.

Instead, head to Mucho Gusto, the second most-hidden restaurant in all of Santa Fe. Although the address notes that it is "on" Paseo de Peralta, a busy loop street that encircles all of downtown Santa Fe, it is actually tucked into a corner of an odd shopping center just off Peralta and past Alameda. It is hard to find but amazing and worth the trouble.

Another place that received a Certificate of Excellence from Trip Advisor, the cozy setting of Mucho Gusto belies the excellent food, pricing, and service offered.

Most of the fare consists of standard Southwest dishes, but all of them are prepared with care, and portions are tasty and generous. However, a few unique selections, like orange tequila shrimp and the queso fundido—a kind of Mexican fondue, contribute something special to the menu.

839 Paseo de Peralta, 505-955-8402
muchogustosantafe.com

TIP:
Don't ever go to Taco Bell in Santa Fe.
You can always do better.

EXPERIENCE THE PAPER(THIN) DOSAS
OF INDIAN CUISINE

Santa Fe is alive with Indian restaurants. Three places immediately come to mind—and if you want an Indian buffet for lunch, India House on Cerrillos Road can't be beat. There is a pop-up, carryout place owned by a gentleman who had a regular and popular restaurant for several years. And then there is Paper Dosa, which features fare from southern India.

At one time, chef Paulraj Karuppasamy and his business partner, Nellie Tischler, did pop-up servings and special events themselves, but in 2015 they opened this always busy, casual-but-elegant restaurant in a semi-out-of-the-way location.

Dosas are like thin crepes made from fermented batter, and many of the restaurant's offerings include them or are based on them.

Paper Dosa is vegetarian friendly and open only for dinner. It has a tasting menu that includes such things as asparagus soup and Chennai chicken, or you can order from the dosa menu, which has eleven offerings. There are also listings for uttapams (a type of Indian "pancake') and curries. My recommendation: the classic masala dosa.

When I finish writing the last entry for this book, I think I know where I am heading to celebrate.

551 W. Cordova Rd., 505-930-5521
paper-dosa.com

SAVOR
A TOUCH OF THE GRAPE

I'm not a wine aficionado, but in my younger years, I drank wine that had soda pop connotations, such as Annie Green Springs and wine spritzers, and I am still trying to figure out why my wife is pleased when she sees that her dinner wine has "legs.'

Santa Fe is the place to learn, with its many wine bars and shops offering opportunities to imbibe in the crush of grapes.

Susan's Fine Wine and Spirits is considered one of the best, with more than a thousand different wines in its store, which also carries other adult imbiberies. It must be doing well, because it has been in business for about fifteen years now.

Gruet Winery has a European heritage and its own vineyard specializing in "Methode Champenoise sparkling wines" in central New Mexico. It has been serving the drink one swirls in New Mexico since the '80s and has sold more than a million bottles of wine.

Susan's Fine Wine and Spirits
1005 S. St. Francis Dr., 505-984-1582
sfwineandspirits.com

Gruet Winery
210 Don Gaspar, 505-989-9463
gruetwinery.com

HAVE
A BARLEY SANDWICH!

Since the popularity of craft beer has risen to amazing levels, it seems that almost every city and town has at least one, if not more, craft breweries.

Santa Fe is no exception, boasting at this writing nearly ten microbreweries, including Second Street Brewing, Santa Fe Brewing, and Tumbleroot, which is also home to a distillery.

Santa Fe Brewing is the oldest, founded in 1988, and has three locations in the city. Unlike most microbreweries, none of these places offers food, but they are often visited by food trucks.

Tumbleroot, on the other hand, does offer food and is one of the newer breweries, opening in 2018.

Second Street Brewery also boasts three sites, all of which have attached restaurants with nicely varied menus.

Other brewhouses in Santa Fe include **Blue Corn**, **Chili Line**, **Rowley Farmhouse Ales**, and **Honeymoon**, which offers a true oddity: artisanal alcoholic kombucha. Hmm . . .

Santa Fe Brewing, multiple locations
santafebrewing.com

Tumbleroot Brewing and Distillery, 2791 Agua Fria, 505-780-5730
tumblerootbreweryanddistillery.com

Second Street Brewery, multiple locations
secondstreetbrewery.com

TIP:
Not familiar with kombucha?
Usually the term refers to a sweet, fermented,
slightly alcoholic, bubbly tea renowned for its
health benefits. It is sometimes called tea to
distinguish it from the original yeast culture
from which it comes.

WATCH FOR CELEBRITIES FROM YOUR PERCH
AT THE TEAHOUSE

The Teahouse, still another winner of Trip Advisor's Certificate of Excellence, is a unique place, on a unique road, in a unique town.

Open daily from 9 a.m. to 9 p.m., it offers chai, coffee, matcha (ground green tea), espresso, cold drinks, and dozens upon dozens of teas, ranging from Japan to rooibos to caffeine-free infusions. It might take a week to decide what to have. It also sells loose tea for home use.

Its food menu, although small and light, consists of things such as polenta Catalan (polenta with roasted veggies and Romano sauce) and includes diverse items such as *posole rojo*, a bacon, roasted pear, and brie panini; and confetti eggs, made with parmesan, tomato, and scallion.

If you need some lighter fare while rambling on Canyon Road, this is certainly the place to be.

821 Canyon Rd., 505-992-0972
teahousesantafe.com

TIP
Don't go to any restaurants that require reservations without a reservation. You'll be disappointed.

SANTA FE TRIVIA

Are you familiar with the actor Jack Palance? Often a character actor, he was the baddest bad guy in *Shane*, played an Old West version of Ebenezer Scrooge in *Ebenezer*, and won an Academy Award for his portrayal of Curly Washburn in the New Mexico comedy, *City Slickers*.

He once lived in Santa Fe as did his daughter, who operated a restaurant on Canyon Road, home of a zillion galleries and few affordable restaurants.

NOT JUST ANOTHER TEQUILA SUNRISE
AT THE SANTA FE MARGARITA TRAIL

The Santa Fe Margarita Trail is a game of sorts but seems rather fun if you are into margaritas. You can use an iPhone or Android to participate, and if you visit enough of the participating bars and cafés, you can even win a prize or two. Drinking responsibly is the key!

Present the app for the Santa Fe Margarita Trail to the barkeep and you will get a buck off each drink. The barkeep can then "stamp" your app, but you can only do two every twelve hours (aha!). After five stamps, you can get a t-shirt (in case you lose yours somewhere along the way), ten or fifteen stamps will gain you entry to the Margarita Society, twenty gets you *The Great Margarita Book* (somewhat less useful than this one is), and thirty gets you a Bartender Kit. Get all forty-five and you win a Margarita VIP package.

Santa Fe Margarita Trail, various locations
santafe.org/margaritatrail

TIP
Start at La Choza because it also has good food to pair with your margarita.

MUSIC AND ENTERTAINMENT

APPRECIATE
REAL CINEMA

New Mexico is well known for its movie industry, which flourishes nowadays because of a desirable incentive program for filmmakers, competent and numerous crew people, and oft-times friendly weather enhanced by regional scenery. Nearly eight hundred films, television shows at least an hour in length, and silent short movies have been at least partially shot in the state since 1897.

But where to go to see some of these cinematic gems?

That's an easy question to answer because of the number of venues in the city, which at one time rivaled New York City in the number of people per capita who attended movies.

The Center for Contemporary Arts's main Cinematheque has two screens and is a non-profit organization. In 2018 it acquired a separate theatre, cleverly named the Screen, from the City of Santa Fe, and this became the CCA's Midtown theater.

All three venues show mostly "arthouse" type films: a mixture of features, documentaries, and foreign offerings. CCA has a main theater and a smaller "side" screen, while the Screen is a rather big hall located on the campus of the now-defunct Santa Fe University of Art and Design.

The Jean Cocteau is a bit of a maverick operation, owned by Game of Thrones author G. R. R. Martin, who lives in Santa Fe and drives a purple Tesla, by the way. This venue was revived by

Martin in 2013 and shows smaller films, peppered with screenings of classic films and numerous other events, as well.

Violet Crown, which is part of a small chain, is the newcomer, featuring eleven screens, a full bar and food menu, and comfy seating. It opened in 2015 and tries not to compete very much with the other small venues. Violet Crown shows a variety of mainstream releases, sprinkled with indie and foreign titles, as well.

CCA
1050 Old Pecos Trail, 505-982-1338
ccasantafe.org

The Screen at Midtown Campus
1600 St. Michael's Dr., 505-428-0209
ccasantafe.org

Jean Cocteau Cinema
418 Montezuma Ave., 505-466-5528
jeancocteaucinema.com

Violet Crown Santa Fe
1606 Alcaldesa St., 505-216-5678
santafe.violetcrown.com

AND SPEAKING OF MOVIES . . .
ATTEND NOT ONE BUT TWO FILM FESTIVALS

Santa Fe is probably the only small city in the United States that has two annual film festivals.

The bigger of the two is the Santa Fe Independent Film Festival. It was begun in 2009 by some filmmakers who were disenchanted with the Santa Fe Film Festival, which at that time was an enormous and successful endeavor. However, over the years, the indie fest has become #1 and is cited by several publications as a worthwhile festival to submit work to. It is held in mid-October each year and is quite progressive.

The Santa Fe Film Festival ran into financial difficulty a few years ago and is just now rebounding from that. It covers a long weekend and currently takes place in February.

Each festival garners guests of note, and both are strongly supported by the community.

Santa Fe Independent Film Festival, 418 Montezuma Ave., #22
505-349-1414, santafeindependentfilmfestival.com

Santa Fe Film Festival, 60 E. San Francisco St., #307
505-216-6063, santafefilmfestival.com

MAKE FILM HISTORY
IN SANTA FE!

Want to make a movie or just see where some really good movies were made? Santa Fe is your place. With a film history that goes back to the silent film era, the Santa Fe area and New Mexico in general has become a movie-making paradise. Santa Fe's first major contribution to the cinematic scene was *The Texas Rangers*, a 1936 Western with Fred MacMurray, which was nominated for an Oscar.

Garson Studios has been home to such titles as *Young Guns II*, *Longmire*, *City Slickers*, and *Iron Man II*. It has sound stages and anything else you could possibly need to create an iconic film.

Santa Fe Studios, a bit smaller and newer, also hosted *Longmire* and *The Ballad of Buster Scruggs*, among many others. It is operated by Lance Hool, who also directed the best movie ever made about the Mexican-American War, *One Man's Hero*. It is also a complete studio and a fascinating place to visit.

Garson Studios, 1600 St. Michael's Dr., 505-670-7678
garsonstudios.com

Santa Fe Studios, 1 Santa Fe Studios Rd., 505-954-2400
santafestudios.com

PICTURE YOURSELF ON THE SET OF A WESTERN
AT EAVES AND BONANZA

Many a Western film has seen life in New Mexico, the aforementioned *Texas Rangers* being the first, but not the last. Eaves Movie Ranch and Bonanza Creek Ranch are still active in the film world and are used often—plus they offer tours.

Eaves was host to a contemporary Western television series, *Empire*, first aired in 1962. Since then, many a film and many a star has set foot on Eaves, which is now "semi-retired," with the last film shoot being the remake of *The Magnificent Seven* in 2016.

Bonanza Creek, however, remains active and is a bit older. It opened its gates with *The Man from Laramie*, starring Jimmy Stewart. This film also has the distinction of being one of a very few allowed to be shot at Taos Pueblo, seventy-five miles or so north of Santa Fe. In more recent years, *Hostiles*, a terrific Western with Christian Bale, used the location and used it well.

Eaves Movie Ranch, 75 Rancho Alegre Rd., 505-474-3045
eavesmovieranch.com

Bonanza Creek Ranch, 15 Bonanza Creek Ln., 505-471-4248
bonanzacreekranch.com

ONE MORE THING:

To finish up our entries on New Mexico's varied film history, the characters from *The Wild Bunch (NOT* shot in New Mexico*)*, quoted below, say it best:

Pike Bishop (William Holden): Let's go!
Lyle Gorch (Warren Oates):
Why the hell not?

CATCH
THE LAST PICTURE SHOW

Back in the good old days, the country was awash with video outlets. You could find VHS tapes for rent at the grocery store or at one of the long-gone chain video stores, such as Hollywood Video and Blockbuster. Now only one still operates in Santa Fe—our amazing Video Library.

Run by Lisa Harris, who also supports various animal rescue groups in Santa Fe, Video Library has an unreal selection of movies, including some that are available only on VHS. And the shop does it all by hand. There is not a computer in the store, nor does it have a website, which proves that sometimes good customer service is all one needs.

The store has been in business since 1981, and of course it isn't making Harris and her husband, Casey St. Charnez, writer and film historian, a lot of money. But they do manage to keep enough people interested in coming back to browse the enormous up-to-date selection.

As for their old-school approach to business, Harris stated in an article published a few years ago that Santa Fe is "a quirky little town" where not everybody, including many of her customers, believes they have to have Wi-Fi buzzing through their homes. She notes, "There are a lot of Luddites like myself. We understand that technology is inevitable, but we don't necessarily embrace and live on it."

839 Paseo de Peralta, 505-983-3321

IMMERSE YOURSELF
IN MUSICA

Since 2004, AMP Concerts has been serving northern New Mexico with numerous shows featuring people of note and some not so noteworthy. Covering Santa Fe, Albuquerque, Taos, and the vicinity, AMP has hosted everyone from the Parson Sisters to Robert Plant (think Led Zeppelin).

Its venues range from public libraries and brewpubs to some of the biggest performance spaces in the state, such as the Santa Fe Opera and Albuquerque's Popejoy Hall.

AMP is a non-profit founded by Neal Copperman, who at one time booked smaller shows and house concerts. Jamie Lenfestey, a long-time local promoter, was added to the staff in 2015, thus ensuring that live music, would continue to be a major draw in Santa Fe and beyond.

AMP also hosts two huge (for New Mexico) events, Globalquerque, a festival of world music and a series of family- and dog-friendly outdoor movies each summer at Santa Fe's beautiful Railyard Park.

AMP Concerts, 505-603-8134
ampconcerts.org

CELEBRATE
MYSTICAL ART

Meow Wolf almost defies definition. First and foremost, it is a family-friendly artsy space, one that turned Santa Fe's renowned art scene on its ear, but it is also a somewhat esoteric outlet for up-and-coming artists and home to small concerts by musicians of all genres.

Founded in 2008, it is an art collective, with the current version housed in a former bowling alley, allowing it thirty thousand square feet of play area. It was funded in part by noted local author George R. R. Martin, writer of the *Game of Thrones* series. Meow Wolf has been so successful that other branches of the space are under construction or due to open soon in Las Vegas, Nevada, and Denver. And at this writing Meow Wolf is heading to Washington, DC, and Phoenix, as well.

Its website notes that "Meow Wolf champions otherness, weirdness, challenging norms, radical inclusion, and the power of creativity to change the world."

1352 Rufina Cir., 505-395-6369
meowwolf.com

DISCOVER
THE CRAWLING, THE FLYING, AND THE CREEPING AT HARRELL HOUSE BUG MUSEUM

Santa Fe is laden with art, cultural, and historical museums—nearly twenty in all. But it is also home to one of the most unique and unusual museums in New Mexico, the Harrell House Bug Museum.

Chock full of more than four thousand arthropods—mounted, not wiggling—and more than 150 live creatures, the Harrell House has something for anyone interested in bugs and spiders and their cousins, including a Hercules beetle, the largest such creature in the world. The museum's live guests include harmless lizards, turtles, snakes, and unusual fish, and there are daily feedings at 4 p.m. Visitors are welcome—to observe, not as dinner!

542 N. Guadalupe (inside DeVargas Center), 505-695-8569
harrellhouse.com

SHUT UP
AND PLAY ALL THE HITS!

Although the transmitter is based in nearby Las Vegas, New Mexico, KBAC 98.1 remains another Santa Fe icon. Its motto, "radio free Santa Fe," is reasonably accurate. Although it is now owned by a small group, KBAC plays a lot of things you may not have heard before and things you heard once or twice in the past and are pleased to hear again after a lapse of too many years.

The station began in 1989 and has gone through various owners. Even the staff tried to purchase the station in 2007, unsuccessfully.

KBAC is community oriented, especially for a commercial station, and its eclectic playlists offer a pleasing variety of music and information, not constant repeats of the same twenty stinky songs like many stations run by conglomerates. And, best of all, most of its programs are hosted by real live people like Honey Harris, who is probably the most real and popular DJ in all of New Mexico.

2502 Camino Entrada, 505-471-1067
santafe.com/kbac

SHOWCASING ART
IN PUBLIC PLACES

You will certainly note as you wander Santa Fe that art is big here. The only things that might surpass it are tourists and chiles (not chili).

In 1985, the city began sponsoring "art in public places," and the project now boasts more than seventy pieces of art of all types scattered about the city. Most of it is part of a permanent collection, so if you go looking for an art installation, chances are you will be able to see it.

Several of the more amazing works of art (again noting that most anything around here can be labeled art) include *Trail of Dreams*, *Trail of Ghosts* by Catherine Widgery, *New Mexico Quilt* by Janet Maher and Marie Stewart, and *El Diferente* by Mac Vaughan, a cool and unique sculpture located at Hillside Park, at Marcy Street and Paseo de Peralta.

It might take a while to view all the pieces (one of which is at the airport, in case you are flying in or out of Santa Fe), but don't miss *Homage to the Burro* by Charles Southard, located just outside the Lensic Theater at where else? Burro Alley.

505-955-6707
santafenm.gov/art_in_public_places

SPEAKING OF ART ...
SEEK OUT THE SANTA FE GALLERY ASSOCIATION

Many people move to Santa Fe for its amazing and unique art world. Some of them are patrons, others collectors, and still others are real artists, and most in the last category hope to make their living via their creations.

That doesn't happen often, but if you hope to have your work in a gallery, Santa Fe is your best bet. With more than two hundred galleries, including many along famed Canyon Road, you could stay busy for weeks just touring them and appreciating or questioning the work of numerous artisans and would-be artists.

There are also numerous galleries in and around downtown and in the newest arts area of the city, the Railyard Arts District.

Want to see work by famous artists? Where to start . . . Santa Fe has been home to such luminaries as Georgia O'Keeffe, Gustave Baumann, Allan Houser, T. C. Cannon, and Bob Haozous.

505-982-1648
santafegalleryassociation.org

GIVE OPERA A CHANCE

Famous enough that Supreme Court Justice Ruth Bader Ginsberg attends, the Santa Fe Opera presents performances every summer in a remarkable and beautiful open-air space, which is a popular spot for pre-opera tailgate gatherings, even using tailgate picnics prepared and sold *at* the opera. This is a place where you can wear jeans and cowperson boots. It also offers electronic language translations and other concerts after the opera season ends.

The Santa Fe Opera is famous for its relaxed atmosphere and most especially for the acoustics. The website notes: "Those acoustics have served a vastly varied and still growing repertory: some two thousand performances of 170 operas by eighty-five composers, including fifteen world premieres, forty-five American premieres, and almost every opera by Richard Strauss."

301 Opera Dr., 505-986-5900
santafeopera.org

BE ENTERTAINED
BY NEW MEXICO POLITICS

Another unique thing about Santa Fe, which is the capital of New Mexico, is that you can explore the state capitol, known as the Roundhouse, no questions asked—either on your own or as part of a tour. It is indeed round, has art galore created by New Mexico artists, and houses our entire legislature, the only one in the country that does not pay its members a salary. Yes, you read that right. All our senators and representatives receive only a $161 per day per diem. This might explain why New Mexico is seen as one of the most backward states, or then again it might show that we are ahead of our time, because these elected folks meet only for thirty days per year in even-numbered years and for sixty days in odd-numbered years.

That said, the Roundhouse is unique and fascinating, and you can watch the tos and fros of the congresspeople from galleries in both the House and Senate rooms. You can carry in a gun, but you can't wear a cap in the galleries. You read it here first. And don't ask me why.

490 Old Santa Fe Trail, 505-986-4589
nmlegis.gov/visitors

MEDITATE
ON THE HAIKU PATHWAY

There are thirty-six haiku stones at this unusual spot, which came to be because of the work of local poet and instructor Miriam Sagan and artist Christy Hengst. The garden stones are made of clay, and each one is hand-stamped with an original haiku set up in a way that allows guests to stop and appreciate each piece.

Sagan noted in an interview that "the clay is so much more integrated with the vision of the pathway here than stone could ever be," adding that "it's softer and it has a slightly more natural or ephemeral feeling. We thought the pieces would look like mushrooms here." Quite.

Santa Fe Community College Courtyard,
6401 Richards Ave., 505-428-1000
sfcc.edu

FEELIN' LUCKY?

Although none is located in Santa Fe proper, the area is dotted with casinos run by various Pueblo Indian groups.

Within an hour's drive, you can visit at least three different tribal casinos. Although somewhat dwarfed in size by the huge competitors on the outskirts of Albuquerque, they offer a full range of ways to entertain yourself for a day or even a long weekend. Take chances, try out the restaurants, overnight in an on-site hotel, or attend a concert. Buffalo Thunder, the biggest casino, offers live entertainment, including nationally known acts and musicians. It is operated by the Pojoaque Pueblo and boasts a Hilton Hotel.

Nearby, for those less inclined to gamble, is the Poeh Cultural Center, a fantastic museum that encompasses the varied cultures of New Mexico's nineteen pueblos. Poeh in the Tewa language translates to "path," which is a good way to describe this brief but interesting view of pueblo history and art.

Buffalo Thunder, 20 Buffalo Thunder Trail, 505-455-5555
hiltonbuffalothunder.com

Poeh Cultural Center, 78 Cities of Gold Rd., 505-455-3334
go-newmexico.com/Poeh-Museum-and-Cultural-Center

LEARN
TO READ THE STARS

One of the most fascinating things about writing this book was learning about places and things around Santa Fe that I had no idea existed—Astronomy Adventures being by far the most exciting.

Operated by Peter Lipscomb, Astronomy Adventures offers one- or two-hour views of the truly amazing New Mexico night sky, unencumbered by city lights.

Lipscomb uses a large Newtonian reflector telescope with a mirror that is twenty inches in diameter. He says that when it is pointed straight up, it shows a lot of detail on the moon, planets, and even star clusters and galaxies that are far, far away.

What you will see, of course, depends on the time of year, the weather, and cloud cover. Lipscomb explains, "Often, we can view some of the planets that share our solar system. Then, there are the deep sky objects. Some of them, like nebulae, supernova remnants, stars and star clusters, are within the Milky Way Galaxy, while other objects are much more distant."

Fifteen miles south of Santa Fe on Hwy. 14, 505-577-7141
astronomyadventures.com

SPORTS AND RECREATION

SKI
RUGGED MOUNTAIN TERRAIN

People who have never been to New Mexico often assume that we live in a climate that is nothing more than deserts with scorpions; Gila monsters; sand dunes; burning, searing temperatures; and saguaro cacti (you know, those big tall ones with "arms" that grow only in Arizona, eastern California, and northern Mexico—not New Mexico). Alas, greenhorn, 'tis not true.

In northern New Mexico, we have four seasons—spring winds, summer sun, autumn color, and—are you ready?—winter! And with that comes some of the best skiing in the region.

Ski Santa Fe is not only a beautiful spot but also a full-service downhill ski operation with lifts and more than eighty trails. (It is snowing like crazy there even as I write this. They've had a mere sixteen inches of snow in the past week.)

Ski Santa Fe is open daily, and of course it offers lessons and a store. The city runs a bus to the area daily for only $10 round trip.

New Mexico State Hwy. 475, 505-982-4429
skisantafe.com

BREAK OUT
THE PEANUTS AND CRACKER JACKS

Like skiing and several other things that seem better suited for more highly populated areas, baseball is not often consider to be part of New Mexico's history.

Well, kinda wrong again, pilgrim, as the state has a history of minor league and semi-professional teams that stretches clear back to the 1920s, when some of the players from the Black Sox Scandal, after being banned from the major leagues, ended up in the Silver City area of New Mexico to continue their careers on a much different level.

Santa Fe can't lay claim to anything of such notoriety, but we do have a Pecos League team called Santa Fe Fuego. The twelve-team league covers four states.

Made up mostly of young players who, in general, aren't signed but want to play ball, the Fuego are Santa Fe's first team and started league play in 2012. There is not a stadium per se, but Fort Marcy Park's diamond has been upgraded and has always been home to the team, which is laid back, often offering high-scoring games and keeping admission and beer prices affordable. What more could one ask for?

505-204-2093
santafefuego.com

FLOAT THROUGH LIFE
ON A RAFT!

Although rafting companies based in Santa Fe need to haul their guests farther upriver to the Taos or Chama area, it is certainly worth the drive.

Santa Fe Rafting offers several different trips, ranging from partial day floats in gentle water to three-day adventures in the Chama area or Class IV rapids in the "Taos Box"; it has the whole spectrum well covered. Each trip includes transportation and a snack. The overnight journeys promise gourmet food, hiking, fishing, and unbelievable scenery.

Kokopelli Rafting Adventures offers a wider range of trips, including a half-day trip and an overnighter to White Rock Canyon that is available year-round. It has designated meeting places where its vans pick up guests and take them to wherever they may be floating. It also offers a guide training school.

Both companies guarantee that you'll get more than your feet wet.

Santa Fe Rafting, 1000 Cerrillos Rd., 505-988-4914
santaferafting.com

Kokopelli Rafting Adventures, 1164 Parkway Dr., Unit A, 505-983-3734
kokopelliraft.com

TIP

Try to visit in the fall. The weather is almost always perfect, there are fewer people, and sometimes it can even save you a few bucks.

HIKE
THE DALE BALL TRAILS

Thanks to the Santa Fe Conservation Trust, this twenty-two-mile system of trails just a tad north of downtown Santa Fe winds its way through the foothills of the Sangre de Cristo Mountains, offering wilderness experiences for novices and experienced hikers alike. Each trail allows for easy navigation because of the unique trail numbering system. The trail network was made possible by the generosity of private landowners, the city, and the county. The park is named after Dale Ball, who was heavily involved in the construction and design.

Two parking lots serve the Dale Ball Trails. One is at the intersection of Hyde Park Road and Sierra del Norte. The other is at the intersection of Upper Canyon Road and Cerro Gordo.

505-989-7019
sfct.org/dale-ball-trails

EXPLORE
NEW MEXICO TERRAIN

Need a break from people and places? This winding route covers about ten miles and follows the sometimes (often) dry Santa Fe River as it meanders through downtown Santa Fe to the New Mexico Highway 599 bypass west of town.

Despite chronic re-construction caused by the weather (storm waters washing away trees and occasional neighborhood overflow), it is still a unique way to explore and experience the terrain of northern New Mexico. The city continues to work on the project, and the brochures promise that "the trail will be one of three primary urban trail spines along with the Rail Trail and Arroyo Chamisa Trail serving the Santa Fe area. The parkway will provide open space corridors, trails for walking and biking, and a series of parks, as well as a way for bicycle commuters to get to and from downtown safely."

1413 Second St., Ste. 3, 505-820-1696
santafewatershed.org

GET YOUR OUTDOOR SELF ON
AT HYDE MEMORIAL STATE PARK

Camping? Hiking? Picnicking?

You can do it all at Hyde Memorial State Park, just a short drive from the Santa Fe Plaza as you head to the ski basin. Winter visitors can also snowshoe, cross-country ski, and even sled. It is also a popular place to take your dog for a walk or hike that will be a good workout for you both.

Hyde was New Mexico's first state park, established in 1938, with elevations from 8,300 to 9,400 feet, and it has a nice lodge for meetings, weddings (*awwww*), and family reunions. It parallels Little Tesuque Creek and offers five well-marked trails ranging in length from just over a quarter of a mile to the more challenging 2.2-mile West Circle Trail for the more advanced hiker. There is some water, but all visitors are cautioned to be properly prepared for anything from quick weather changes (this is mountain country, y'know) to a possible critter encounter. No bears, but there are deer, fox, a multitude of birds, porcupines (watch where you sit), and maybe even a Yeti . . .

740 Hyde Park Rd., 505-983-7175
emnrd.state.nm.us

TIP

For a new adventure, reserve one of the
yurts in the park. No electricity, but there
are fire rings, propane heaters, and beds.
You'll need to bring your own chuck, bedding,
and cooking gear. Leave the darn cellphone
at home, por favor!

WANDER NEW MEXICO

Think you'll get hungry while wandering Santa Fe or want to sample a variety of vittles offered in the City Different?

Wander New Mexico offers just the solution—a choice of reasonably short walking tours of the city, all of which stop at various places of gastronomical delight. You can also arrange for a custom or private tour.

The "Off the Beaten Path" tour takes place in the Railyard Arts District, offering (depending on the day) selections of food such as a tartine from Sage Bakehouse, a chef's choice at Joseph's of Santa Fe, or a green chile cheeseburger from the Second Street Brewery.

Not to your liking? How about "Sip and Savor" on the historic plaza, offering a taco tasting at El Callejon, a chef's choice at the world-famous Coyote Café, or from Sazon a sampling of mole (chocolate-chile sauce) and mezcal?

Perhaps the most interesting, which offers a lighter bill o' fare—wine and cheese—is the "Women of the West" jaunt, which offers information about the Harvey Girls; pioneer woman Susan Shelby Magoffin; and Doña Tules, a saloon owner nicknamed the "queen of sin."

Tours vary in length, are offered rain or shine, and can even accommodate vegetarians and those with gluten issues.

505-395-0552
wandernewmexico.com

TOUR SANTA FE
ON TWO WHEELS

Sadly, it is nearly impossible to get to Santa Fe except by car. The Rail Runner drops people off at semi-inconvenient places, and the city bus system, although well-meaning, can be a bit slow and not terribly reliable for people on a schedule.

However, once you *do* get here, there are other options, including a bike tour.

Santa Fe Biking Tours is operated by Roger Mui, whose wife, Carol, operates Historic Walks of Santa Fe. Mui's bike tours are essentially "custom" designed and last about three hours each. Mui offers hybrid lightweight bikes, helmets, and a comfortable pace. The tours offer a complete review of the city, from architecture to art, and they are available year-round.

608 E. Palace Ave., 505-690-0626
santafebikingtours.com

GO SOAK YOUR HEAD
IN A HOT SPRING POOL

It is not immediately apparent why New Mexico has so many hot spring pools, but there are several of them scattered throughout the state.

Santa Fe proper has two, Sunrise Springs and Ten Thousand Waves, both of which offer public and private soaks.

Sunrise Springs is operated by the same folks who tend to nearby Ojo Caliente, about an hour away. Sunrise Springs is in a beautiful setting and has a wonderful restaurant, complemented by a tasteful little gift shop. It also offers lodging.

Ten Thousand Waves offers accommodations, a superb Japanese restaurant, and a small gift shop.

And if you travel around the state, you will also be able to soak your aching bones at Jemez Springs, rural Faywood, and Truth or Consequences, formerly known as, well, Hot Springs.

Sunrise Springs, 242 Los Pinos Rd., 505-780-8145
sunrisesprings.ojospa.com

Ten Thousand Waves, 21 Ten Thousand Waves Way, 505-982-9304
tenthousandwaves.com

VISIT
THE HISTORIC WALKS OF SANTA FE

With a lot to see and do in Santa Fe, Historic Walks of Santa Fe is something that everyone should consider. Owner Carol Mui offers an array of custom tours of the City Different, ranging from culinary tours to "ghostwalkers." Mui also offers out-of-town tours to Taos, Bandelier National Monument, and the historic village of Chimayo.

Each stroll is unique, and as added bonuses Mui offers Spanish translation and the opportunity to bring your favorite dog along for some good exercise.

608 E. Palace Ave., 505-986-8388
historicwalksofsantafe.com

TIP
If you go to a ceremony or feast at a pueblo, obey their rules.
You are a guest on their land.

HAVE AN AUTHENTIC WESTERN ADVENTURE
ON HORSEBACK

Don't feel like biking or walking? How about getting your muscles in an uproar and taking a one- or two-hour horseback ride in a beautiful area south of Santa Fe called the Turquoise Trail?

Based at a ranch that has been in the same family for more than sixty years, Santa Fe Western Adventures does recommend that only "frequent or experienced riders should take part in the two-hour ride, but novices are welcome on the shorter route and the glorious sunset ride as well."

If you fit the bill, you can see things that you would not have the chance to see on your own, including some sites where movies and television shows were filmed and a small cave, all located on the private ranch.

As John Steinbeck once said, "A man on a horse is spiritually, as well as physically, bigger than a man on foot."

Lone Butte Ranch, 505-473-9384
santafewest.com

CULTURE AND HISTORY

MAKE A WISH
WHEN YOU ENTER
THIS PLACE OF WORSHIP

Dating from 1610, the opulent and amazing Cathedral Basilica of St. Francis of Assisi guards the east end of Santa Fe's famed plaza. The current structure was built in 1887 and has seen several upgrades since. There are no tours per se, but the website has a virtual tour, and serious people of faith are welcome to attend a service and perhaps take a quick look around afterward.

The church holds daily Masses, and according to the church website, "the Cathedral was elevated to a Basilica by Pope Benedict XVI in 2005. Basilica denotes a church of particular importance in Rome and abroad. Churches are honored by the Holy Father because of their importance in the history of spreading Catholicism."

131 Cathedral Pl., 505-982-5619
cbsfa.org

SCHEDULE YOUR DREAM WEDDING
AT THE LORETTO CHAPEL

An immediate neighbor to the Cathedral Basilica, the famed Loretto Chapel—a lovely former church that is now a museum and wedding chapel—is a trifle more tourist-friendly, shall we say, than the cathedral. Its website promotes it as a wedding venue (no thanks, three times was enough for me), and the online gift shop offers everything from Loretto Chapel Christmas tree ornaments to copies of the movie The Staircase that was made for television in 1998. It tells the story of the famed staircase that is considered a miraculous bit of architecture because of its circular design, two 360-degree turns, and the use of only wooden pegs to hold it together.

A line from the movie *The Man Who Shot Liberty Valance* says it best: "When the legend becomes fact, print the legend." Nonetheless, it is a beautiful staircase in a stunning setting.

207 Old Santa Fe Trail, 505-982-0092
lorettochapel.com

VISIT
THE SITE OF JAPANESE INTERNMENT

During World War II, an internment camp was set up near Santa Fe to hold men of Japanese American descent who were thought to be "high risk." Located north of downtown near what is now the Santa Fe National Cemetery, the camp housed as many as 4,500 "alien enemies," some of whom were held for months after the war ended.

After news of the Bataan Death March surfaced, a mob of angry citizens descended on the camp, but the commander convinced them that abuse of the Japanese would only lead to abuse of American POWs, and the crowd dispersed. On the other hand, a man named Detweiler from New York attempted to convince authorities in 1942 to allow a colony of Japanese farmers to live and work freely near Maxwell, New Mexico, about one hundred miles northeast of Santa Fe. It was, of course, never allowed. There is now a memorial plaque in remembrance of the camp.

Japanese Internment Camp Remembrance Site, 1474 La Loma Vista

BE A TEMPORARY LOCAL
IN THE PLAZA (NOT PLAYA)

Even though Santa Fe's Plaza is pretty much world famous, at least to those folks who know that New Mexico is a state, it certainly bears mention here.

Many New Mexico cities and towns have plazas, but ours has a vibrant, welcoming atmosphere. It is a four-hundred-year-old gathering place for events of all kinds, and when it is event-free it is a pleasant respite for those exploring the shops that surround the plaza, of which only a few are chains.

A bandstand on the north side often features bands and local acts, and at Christmas time the place is decorated with thousands of tiny lights.

And if you are a carnivore, indulge in a Frito "pie," at the nearby Five and Dime General Store before checking out its extensive collection of tchotchkes.

Another nice thing about the plaza is that it offers high-end goods alongside the t-shirt of your dreams.

100 Old Santa Fe Trail, 800-777-2489
santafe.org

BE SEEN, BUT NOT HEARD
AT THE SANTA FE CHILDREN'S MUSEUM

Children who visit the Santa Fe Children's Museum must be accompanied by an adult, but don't be surprised if the kids have to push you out of the way while you are playing with the hands-on exhibits.

The museum has classes ranging from recycled art projects to culinary training and most everything in between. The exhibits often change, and there is even the Stargazer Portable Planetarium, a cool high-definition "traveling" host that offers "cultural tales, star talks, and interplanetary travel." The museum also occasionally offers a Sensory Friendly Morning for little tykes who have autism or sensory sensitivities.

If you need a break from the kiddos, the museum offers camps, but if you really love being with your kids, you can rent the facility for a sleepover.

Plus, it has the second-best gift shop in the city (right after Doodlet's), not to mention Cornelius the Corn Snake . . . a super-friendly fellow.

1050 Old Pecos Trail, 505-989-8359
santafechildrensmuseum.org

TIP

No need to bring your passport.
New Mexico is a state, sandwiched between
Texas and Arizona. We became a state rather
late in life, 1912, but we are a state, even though
it doesn't seem like it sometimes. Our population
is a smidge over two million, thirty-sixth
in the union.

INDULGE IN HOT WAX ART
AT THE MUSEUM OF ENCAUSTIC ART

I'd never heard of encaustic art until I stumbled on the Museum of Encaustic Art, a unique private museum operated by the Encaustic Art Institute.

Encaustic art dates back to the first century BC and uses heated wax to which colored pigments are added. The wax can be used on paper, wood, or canvas to create a type of photography, paintings, and even sculpture. It creates a unique and colorful type of fine art.

The museum was founded in 2005 in the small community of Cerrillos outside of Santa Fe. Owners Douglas and Adrienne Mehrens moved the museum to a larger location in Santa Fe in 2015.

Besides housing the world's largest exhibits of the art, the museum offers workshops, classes for all ages, and juried exhibitions.

Santa Fe is loaded with museums, but none quite like this one.

632 Agua Fria St., 505-989-3283
moeart.org

TOUR
(ONE OF) THE OLDEST HOUSES
IN THE UNITED STATES (?)

Built upon the foundation of a Pueblo Indian ruin, this little place once labeled itself the oldest house in the United States. Taking into account that First Nation's people have been here for millenniums, the claim of course refers to European-style buildings. Therefore, it is probably not the oldest house, but it is pretty darn old.

The foundation dates back to 1200 AD, with "tree-ring specimens, taken from some of the vigas (indoor roof support beams) in the ceilings of the lower rooms, [which] show cutting dates of 1740–1767." In the early 1700s, it was also a temporary home for the territorial governor, when repairs were being made to the structure of the nearby San Miguel Church. There is also a small museum connected with the house and admission is free.

There are numerous very old structures in New Mexico (including me): Taos Pueblo, Acoma Pueblo, and the Palace of the Governors, not to mention that very same San Miguel Church compound which has been in use for more than four hundred years.

215 E. DeVargas St., 505-988-1944
historicsantafe.org/the-oldest-house

TRAVEL
THE OLD EL CAMINO REAL

Even older than Route 66 is El Camino Real, which carried traders, goods, and people from Mexico City north through what is now El Paso, Texas, terminating just north of Santa Fe at the San Juan Pueblo.

The 1,600-mile road was used from before the year 1000 until about 1882 and is now a UNESCO World Heritage Site in Mexico, with any number of markers listing bits of information about it scattered throughout New Mexico. At times, locations that were used as campsites for many years were later turned into towns such as Socorro and Albuquerque. For the most part, the road ran parallel to the Rio Grande, which of course offered a necessary water source for many miles. In Santa Fe proper, several markers commemorate the road, which runs roughly along Agua Fria Street to the Plaza.

505-954-2000
blm.gov/visit/el-camino-real-nht

GET YOUR KICKS
ON ROUTE 66

From 1926 to 1937, the original path of beloved Route 66 went through Santa Fe after veering off course in the town of Santa Rosa and heading north to Pecos. It then dropped south through Bernalillo before going through to Albuquerque.

However, in one of the more interesting political ploys in the state, the outgoing governor of New Mexico, Arthur T. Hannett, decided to "get even" after getting the proverbial boot in the recent election.

Hannett issued an edict before leaving office that a state highway be built from Santa Rosa to Moriarty, both small towns south and east of Santa Fe on what became a stretch of 66. It was built in record time—before Hannett left office—but it took another ten years for it to become part of Route 66. It was just a dirt road, but it was straight and cut Santa Fe off, leaving the capital a bit high and dry. However, in the end, Hannett did everyone a favor because a dangerous part of the old route, south of Santa Fe, then became obsolete.

Various signs around the city point out the original route, with a historical marker about ten miles northeast on what is now known as the Old Las Vegas Highway.

route66guide.com

IS IT TRUE
ABOUT THE OTHER ALIENS?

New Mexico folklore is rife with UFO and alien stories. All such reports are pure hokum, especially the Roswell UFO incident, but they do make for good tourist fodder.

Several hundred UFO sightings have been reported and logged, most especially on the funny website nuforc.org, which includes an entry about a 1972 UFO sighting in northern New Mexico, with the witness adding, "Out of Body Experience not caused by drugs!" There are no known out-of-this-world beings in Santa Fe—but wait . . . what is that blinking light outside my office window? Could it be . . . ?

TIP

If you feel like a drive, visit the International UFO Museum and Research Center in Roswell, NM, three hours south of Santa Fe, for out-of-this-world entertainment.

114 N. Main St., Roswell, 575-625-9495

LOOK FOR FACT, NOT FICTION
AT THE NEW MEXICO MILITARY MUSEUM

Although not well known outside of the state, New Mexico and of course Santa Fe has an amazing military history.

Much of it comes from the greed for land. The Mexican-American War, fought in the 1840s, included the Battle of Santa Fe—which wasn't really a battle. During the Civil War, Santa Fe was briefly occupied by the Confederate Army until it was defeated at nearby Glorieta, with a body count from both sides of nearly one hundred.

The New Mexico Military Museum covers these conflicts and offers extensive information and displays about the Battle of Bataan and the ensuing "Death March," as many of the American soldiers who were caught up in that horrific experience were members of the 200th and 515th Coast Artillery, based in New Mexico.

The museum is small but packs a powerful punch with its exhibits, which include some vehicles, most of a World War I airplane, and a helicopter used in Vietnam.

1050 Old Pecos Trail, 505-238-5086
bataanmuseum.com

PICK UP A SECOND HOUSE:
CERRO PELON RANCH

Care to own you own movie set? Here's your chance. The Western "town" that was used to shoot *Silverado* (1984), *Lonesome Dove* (1980), and the non-Western *Thor* (2015), among others, is for sale. As a bonus, along with the town, you also get the twenty-thousand-acre (thirty-two-square-mile) Cerro Pelon (Bald Hill) Ranch, which offers a reflecting pool that magnificently mirrors the main house, an office building, three other houses, indoor and outdoor horse arenas, a tennis court, and an airstrip.

Currently owned by clothing designer Tom Ford, who purchased it in 2001, the place was originally owned by Montana ranchers Marian and Bill Cook and is somewhat environmentally sensitive to boot.

At this writing, it has been on the market since 2016 and will only set you back a paltry $75 million. Private tours of the movie set can sometimes be arranged.

Kevin Bobolsky Group, 505-470-6263
kevinbobolskygroup.com/cerro-pelon-ranch-php

ADD TO YOUR LIFE LIST
AT THE RANDALL DAVEY AUDUBON CENTER AND SANCTUARY

Open Monday through Saturday, this small but active place boasts nearly two hundred species of birds that visit, nest, or live year-round in the sanctuary. Although the center's schedule is replete with events and lectures, the sanctuary is also a great place to find some peace and quiet and take short hikes.

The site was purchased from the Martinez family, which had operated a gristmill there since 1852. Prior to that, it was a sawmill that was used to cut wood for the construction of Fort Marcy beginning in 1847. Randall Davey made it into his home and studio in 1920, but it was gifted by the Davey family to the Audubon Society in 1983 after he died and now hosts more than ten thousand guests each year.

1800 Upper Canyon Rd., 505-983-4609
randalldavey.audubon.org

STUDY
NEW MEXICO HISTORY
IN A NEW MUSEUM

The newest in a plethora of museums that dot Santa Fe, the New Mexico History Museum holds its own as the only state-operated museum in the city that doesn't have art as its main attraction.

New Mexico has a unique history that starts at least twelve thousand years ago, with evidence that the Clovis people occupied the area at the end of the last Ice Age. Since then, we have seen the settlement of the Pueblo people and the invasion by the Spanish in the 1500s, with indications that a slave, Estevan the Moor, was the first person of African descent to set foot in New Mexico.

The History Museum is also home to the Palace Press, is part of the timeless Palace of the Governors, houses the state's photo archives, and—perhaps best of all—hosts the "portal Native American Artisans Program" wherein vendors from New Mexico's First Nations tribes and Pueblos sell beautiful and reasonably priced jewelry and small artworks under the portal of the Palace of the Governors every day, rain, snow, or shine.

113 Lincoln Ave., 505-476-5100
nmhistorymuseum.org

WATCH THE SUNSET
FROM CROSS OF THE MARTYRS PARK

Do you like sunsets, piña coladas, and strolls on the beach? Santa Fe can provide the first two, in particular the sunset part. A great viewing place for sunsets and sunrises is the Cross of the Martyrs Park, a hilltop just a bit northeast of the famed plaza. A high spot with a commanding view westward, it is close to Prince Park, where Fort Marcy was built in the mid-1800s. The fort was "a symbol of American military control" after New Mexico, then a territory, was ceded to the United States via the still hotly debated 1848 Treaty of Guadalupe Hidalgo, which put an end to the Mexican-American War.

The cross itself is a monument to the more than twenty Franciscan friars who were killed in the 1680 Pueblo Revolt. And if you aren't into hill climbing, you can also reach the park by auto via nearby Artist's Road. This is one of fifteen parks in Santa Fe.

617 Paseo de Peralta, 505-955-2500
santafenm.gov

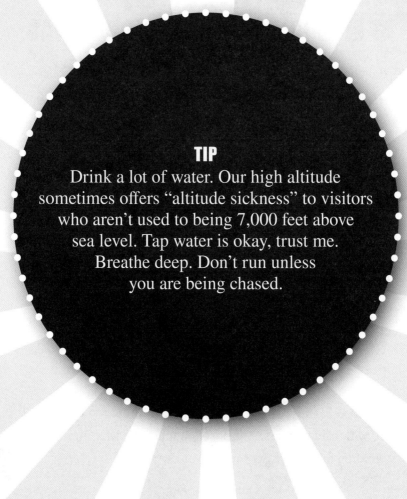

TIP
Drink a lot of water. Our high altitude
sometimes offers "altitude sickness" to visitors
who aren't used to being 7,000 feet above
sea level. Tap water is okay, trust me.
Breathe deep. Don't run unless
you are being chased.

DANCE IT UP
AT EL RANCHO DE LAS GOLONDRINAS

El Rancho de las Golondrinas, which covers two hundred acres a bit south of Santa Fe, was opened in 1972, but some of the colonial buildings on the site date back to the early 1700s.

The museum, whose name translates roughly to "ranch of the swallows," offers living history along with information on the culture and heritage of New Mexico in the eighteenth and nineteenth centuries.

Docents and "villagers" in period clothing offer information on everything from weaving and cooking to blacksmithing and other crafts of the time period.

There are several weekend-long festivals at Golondrinas, including a Harvest Festival, Herb and Lavender Festival, Fiesta de los Niños (children), and even a Renaissance Faire (though it's unlikely that any knights in shining armor were ever seen in New Mexico).

It also has a great little gift shop and offers food and drink, along with private tours. The Josefina tour tells what life was like for children in 1820s New Mexico.

334 Los Pinos Rd., 505-471-2261
golondrinas.org

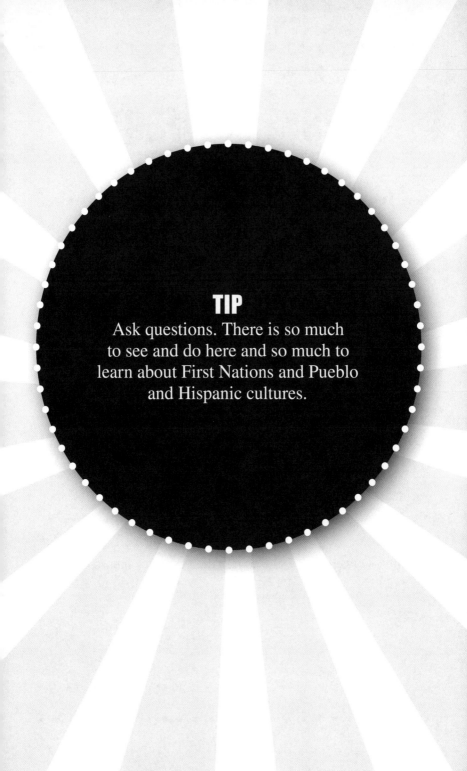

TIP
Ask questions. There is so much
to see and do here and so much to
learn about First Nations and Pueblo
and Hispanic cultures.

PERUSE ARTIFACTS
OF INDIAN ARTS AND CULTURE

New Mexico is home to twenty-three American Indian tribes, including the smaller bands of Pueblo people (eighteen) and five sovereign nations: the Zuni, two tribes of Apache (Inde), Ute, and Dine (Navajo).

The Museum of Indian Arts and Culture is a fascinating and expressive museum featuring art created by many people of those cultures, along with other Southwestern artists.

Included are exhibits of pottery, jewelry, clothing, baskets, and archaeological collections, not to mention contemporary art and a collection donated by instructor Dorothy Dunn of works done by students at the Santa Fe Indian School.

There are also any number of special events, including tribal dances, and a unique and interesting café. The gift shop art is all verified to have been made by Native craftspeople, and the shop also has a wide variety of books.

The location is on "Museum Hill," a short drive from downtown, where you will also find the next three museums.

710 Camino Lejo, 505-476-1269
miaclab.org

MARVEL AT THE SKILL OF NATIVE AMERICAN JEWELERS
AT THE WHEELWRIGHT

It is interesting to note that several states that have larger populations of American Indians, such as Wyoming, Montana, and Utah, don't really have any museums dedicated to American Indian history, culture, and art. New Mexico, which has always been conscious of, although not always kind to, its Native people, has close to ten.

The Wheelwright, one of the oldest and most complete of its kind, was founded in 1937 and is the state's oldest independent museum.

The curators support shows for up-and-coming Native artists, offer exhibits of historical and contemporary art, and are known for their work, which focuses on "little-known genres.'

The Jim and Lauris Phillips Center for the Study of Southwestern Jewelry, which is thought to be the most complete collection of work by Navajo and Pueblo artists in the world, is also housed here.

The Wheelwright is also home to the Case Trading Post, which opened nearly fifty years ago and offers both new and vintage art, jewelry, textiles, and ceramics.

704 Camino Lejo, 505-982-4636
wheelwright.org

PREPARE TO BE AWED
BY SPANISH COLONIAL ART

Moving right along on Museum Hill, our next stop is the Museum of Spanish Colonial Art.

The museum has an interesting history and operates under the auspices of the Spanish Colonial Arts Society, which was started by writer Mary Austin and writer and artist Frank Applegate in 1925. The museum is an offshoot of that.

Their stated goal was to "preserve and perpetuate the Hispano art forms that have been produced in New Mexico and southern Colorado since the region was colonized by Spain in 1598, and to educate the public about these art forms and the art of all the Spanish colonies."

That mission has been successful as the museum closes in on its one-hundredth anniversary. It is the only museum of its type, and it also sponsors the successful and popular Traditional Spanish Market that takes place annually in downtown Santa Fe. The institution itself is home to more than 3,700 contemporary and vintage works, housed in a building designed by John Gaw Meem, a Brazilian-born architect who is considered one of the principals in the founding of the "Pueblo Revival" style of architecture that permeates Santa Fe. Meem and his wife, Faith, were also benefactors of the museum and donated several hundred items to the facility.

750 Camino Lejo, 505-982-2226
spanishcolonial.org

DELVE INTO
INTERNATIONAL FOLK ART

Our last stop on Museum Hill, the Museum of International Folk Art, doesn't really have anything to do with a particular culture, but rather it embraces many cultures.

As the name indicates, this unique and completist museum offers folk art of all kinds from around the world. It is also host to one of the city's biggest yearly events—the International Folk Art Market, held each July. It claims to be the biggest in the world, and in 2019 it hosted one thousand artists from one hundred countries. It is incredibly popular and well worth the cover charge to get in.

As the sponsoring museum, MIFA itself houses more than 130,000 pieces, with the core number of 2,500 donated by collector and museum founder Florence Dibell Bartlett.

Of course, there are rotating exhibits, permanent displays, and something for everyone, from Japanese woodblocks to ceramics from Turkey.

Take the opportunity to browse the collection—it might take a day or two to see it all. It is well worth the price of admission—$7, at the most.

706 Camino Lejo, 505-476-1200
moifa.org

WHILE YOU'RE IN THE NEIGHBORHOOD...
VISIT THE SANTA FE BOTANICAL GARDEN

This small but user-friendly place is situated just across the street from Museum Hill. Open daily from April through October and from Wednesday through Sunday the rest of the year, the botanical garden offers a unique exploratory visit to the world of plants that thrive (usually!) in the area.

The garden has been around for more than twenty years and offers guests several unique experiences, including the "Eyes and Hands Garden" that is centered around a small plaza and offers visitors views of plants that are used for medicine, food, weaving, and dyeing.

Nearby is the largest area of the park, encompassing eight acres: the Arroyo Trails, with a view of arroyo restoration (a hot topic in New Mexico nowadays), along with a pretty diverse group of plants and mammals.

The Museum Hill Bicycle Trail is short—less than a mile—but offers the most spectacular views of the garden's variety of "residents."

725 Camino Lejo, 505-471-9103, santafebotanicalgarden.org

TIP

At Christmas time, the Santa Fe Botanical
Garden is host to a lovely and lively event called
"GLOW," a festival of winter lights
and holiday cheer.

WALK AMONG THE BEST
OF CONTEMPORARY NATIVE ARTS

I've known since the '60s when I first visited that Santa Fe was an art haven, but how much so I didn't really realize until I began exploring this fantastic town to write this book.

Just off downtown, the Museum of Contemporary Arts is part of the world-renowned Institute of American Indian Arts, which has a campus on the far south side of the city.

The institution itself is housed in a beautiful old pueblo-style building, in keeping with the ambiance of its collection. The museum opened in 1972 and in general offers mostly work from contemporary Native American artists, boasting 7,500 pieces within its walls. There are four galleries and an art park named after one of the state's best-known artists, Allan Houser (Apache). The galleries rotate works of art by "national and international cutting-edge contemporary" Native artists. The collection was started in 1961 and includes work from other well-known Native artists, such as Kevin Red Star (Crow), Earl Biss (Crow), T. C. Cannon (Kiowa/Caddo), and Helen Hardin (Santa Clara). Biss, Cannon, and Hardin all passed away at a young age before their work was really recognized.

108 Cathedral Pl., 888-922-4242
iaia.edu/iaia-museum-of-contemporary-native-arts

SOMETHING FOR EVERYONE
AT EL MUSEO CULTURAL DE SANTA FE

A small but important museum located in the Santa Fe Railyard Arts District, El Museo Cultural de Santa Fe is a center for Hispanic culture and learning and is dedicated to promoting the Hispano art, culture, and traditions of Northern New Mexico.

It is also one of the newest entries into the wide world of museum life in Santa Fe, opening "only" twenty years ago. More of an events venue than an actual museum, El Museo offers a seasonal (October to May) market of goods made by international artisans and hosts several concerts, lectures, and workshops pertaining to the community of the native Hispano population of northern New Mexico.

El Museo also offers rotating exhibits by artists in several small but vital gallery spaces, and one of its bigger events of the year relates to altars created for El Día de los Muertos (Day of the Dead), the traditional Mexican celebration that takes place just after Halloween.

555 Camino de la Familia, 505-992-0591
elmuseocultural.org

FOCUS ON INTERNATIONAL ART
AT THE RALPH T. COE CENTER

This non-profit and private museum, which offers free tours by appointment or on the first Friday of each month, was founded by Ralph Coe. He focused on the art of indigenous people, collecting more than 2,200 works from around the world.

On the website, one First Nations artist is quoted as saying that Coe was "accommodating; he was easy to be with, laughed and just went with the flow without too much fanfare. He was humble."

The Coe collection specializes in three areas. The African collection includes nearly two hundred works, from an Ekoi headdress circa the late 1800s to earrings made by the Fulani people. The Oceanic collection offers a battle hammer from the Fijian people dating back to the 1850s. The Native American collection is the largest with about 1,700 pieces, ranging from a whimsical beaded belt buckle featuring a Teenage Mutant Ninja Turtle (made by an Assiniboine artist in Montana) to a wool, silk, and beaded hood from the late 1800s made by a Mi'kmaq artist from Canada.

Ralph T. Coe Center, 1590 B Pacheco St., 505-983-6372
coeartscenter.org

CELEBRATE
A NEW MEXICO ART ICON

One of the more famous artists to land in Santa Fe was the highly praised Georgia O'Keeffe. Born in Wisconsin in 1887, she later taught art in South Carolina and West Texas.

Her first trip to New Mexico was in 1929, and she found the landscape, architecture, and "distinct indigenous art" to be inspiring. She spent the next twenty years living part-time in New Mexico.

After the death of her husband, photographer Alfred Stieglitz, O'Keeffe came here to stay, and her work began to depict what she admired in the landscape. She maintained a home and studio in the small town of Abiquiu, about an hour north of Santa Fe, and lived on and off in Santa Fe proper. She passed away in 1986 at the age of ninety-eight.

The Georgia O'Keeffe Museum is all O'Keeffe, all the time. Within are nine galleries featuring more than seven hundred of her drawings, along with many of the materials she used, photographs, and personal belongings. The exhibits do change, so the museum always deserves a look no matter how many times you visit Santa Fe.

The museum is open daily, and arrangements can also be made to visit her home and studio in Abiquiu. Of course, the museum features a small gift store.

217 Johnson St., 505-946-1000
okeeffemuseum.org

CLEANSE YOUR BAD JUJU
AT THE BURNING OF ZOZOBRA

One of the biggest non-art gatherings in Santa Fe is the annual burning of Zozobra, or "old man gloom."

Sponsored by the local Kiwanis Club, it was started in 1924 by artist Will Shuster, who created the first version of Zozobra, a six-foot puppet, as part of a private party in his backyard for friends. Zozobra was based on a Holy Week celebration of the Yaqui Indian tribe.

It has now morphed into a fifty-foot effigy made of paper and muslin, which is burned (à la the much newer Burning Man event in Nevada) as part of the Santa Fe pageant, which celebrates (sort of) the history of Santa Fe.

In 1964, Shuster turned Zozobra over to the Kiwanis organization, and it is now a community event that benefits kids through scholarships and grants.

The event is big enough that a lot of businesses close early to allow employees and their families to attend the burning, which is said to help people cleanse themselves of bad juju and difficult times. Zozobra is an ugly and wicked character, so it is nice to see something evil go up in smoke.

Fort Marcy Park, 1-855-ZOZOBRA
burnzozobra.com

SHOP AND SOCIALIZE
AT YE OLDE INDIAN MARKET

The Santa Fe Indian Market, which hasn't missed a year since 1922, is yet another nod to the numerous American Indian artists who populate the area, let alone the rest of the nation. It is now among the five largest events in Santa Fe, and each summer it draws guests and artists from everywhere.

The entire city participates, with galleries showing new work by Native artists, cafés offering foods of Native origin, and a small film festival screening works by or for First Nations peoples. The event also includes a fashion show, panel discussion, auction, music and dance, and awards to artists for best in show.

In 2019, nearly one thousand artists will represent more than two hundred recognized tribes, with the number of visitors expected to reach "a lot."

Downtown Plaza, 505-983-5220
swaia.org

TRY UNUSUAL PAIRINGS
AT THE WINE AND CHILE FIESTA

Pop quiz! Winner gets a copy of my next book, which is about where nudists put their cellphones. Ready? Is a chile a fruit or a vegetable?

That question and many others could be answered at the late fall Wine and Chile Fiesta, which is certainly one unique event.

Guest chef demonstrations, sommelier (six at last count)-hosted wine seminars, an auction, food and drink tastings, a golf tournament, and perhaps even a film or two all take place during this slightly highbrow event, which is now closing in on its third decade.

It was a one-day event when it began in 1991. Then, you could buy a coupon book with ten options for a food or wine tasting at various restaurants and wineries.

From that humble beginning, it has grown to an eight-day (and night). You can still get food and wine samples, but now there are a hundred or so wineries participating, with nearly fifty wine-pairing dinners.

The trivia answer? Chile, as spelled here, rather than the ubiquitous chili, is a fruit because it has "internal edible seeds." Chiles are also—supposedly—not eaten by any mammal other than humanoids, with the hottest said to be from Trinidad: the 7 Pot Douglah. It is brown, small, and perhaps a bit like a miniature inferno in one's mouth.

217 E. Marcy, 505-438-8060
santafewineandchile.org

TEST YOUR STAMINA
AT THE GREEN CHILE
CHEESEBURGER SMACKDOWN

A newer entry into Santa Fe's wide, wide world of festivals is the Green Chile Cheeseburger Smackdown. As mentioned throughout the book, chiles, in particular those of the long green variety, are used in every possible permutation in the state, from ice cream to license plates.

This competition features one of the area's more sought-after foods, a cheeseburger with—you guessed it!—green chile. So popular is this unique food item that the Albuquerque Isotopes minor league baseball team reinvents itself as the Green Chile Cheeseburgers a couple of times a year. There is even a "green chile cheeseburger trail," which winds its way around the state, with twenty-one recommended spots from rural Reserve to sorta rural Clovis and from Las Cruces (motto: we're bigger than Santa Fe) to Taos.

But now, thanks to *Edible Magazine*, the Smackdown takes place once a year, with each year's "Chomp" (get it?) receiving an award and a load of publicity. A panel of lucky judges, usually numbering six, chooses the winner of the competition.

So if you happen to be in town in early September, check out this once-a-year and maybe once-in-a-lifetime event, which drew around eight hundred guests in 2018.

505-375-1329
ediblesmackdown.com

SPONSOR A NEW ARTIST
AT THE SPANISH MARKET

Somewhat smaller in scope but no less important than the Indian Market, the twice-yearly Traditional Spanish Market features many Hispano artists, who gather on the plaza in Santa Fe every summer and again in the winter (inside) to share and sell their wares.

The market is sponsored and presented by the Spanish Colonial Arts Society, the same group that operates the Museum of Spanish Colonial Art. The group hosts both adult and youth artists, who present work in eighteen different categories. There are various versions of carved wooden santos (saints), weaving, furniture, jewelry, tinwork, and colcha (an enhanced form of mending).

Youth Market artists are mentored by adult artists in each category, and many of them rely on their art as their only source of income.

Viva la Cultura is a week-long event culminating with the market. It includes music, studio tours, food offerings and events, lectures, and a special "Market Mass" at the Cathedral Basilica of St. Francis.

Santa Fe Plaza, 505-982-2226
spanishcolonial.org

SIP N' SLURP
AT THE SOUPER BOWL

A delicious and unique fundraiser for the Santa Fe Food Depot, which served almost four-hundred thousand meals to people in need last year, is this annual fun and crazy event, held in mid-winter.

Nearly twenty-five restaurants competed in the latest edition of the fund-raising contest, in four categories: vegetarian, seafood, savory, and cream, with a grand prize being awarded as well.

Soup aficionados vote for their favorites as they wander the city convention center in search of the elusive green pea and banana recipe or perhaps look for cream of cream or weasel noodle.

The event just registered its twenty-fifth anniversary, with interest and crowds growing every year.

Santa Fe Convention Center, 201 W. Marcy St., 505-471-1633
thefoodepot.org/souper-bowl

SALUTE
ONE MORE EPHEMERAL EVENT

Santa Fe's love of celebration certainly extends to the Fourth of July and starts early in the morning and extends late into the night.

"Pancakes on the Plaza" starts at 7 a.m. The event is nearly fifty years old and is sponsored by the Rotary Club of Santa Fe. The menu is reasonably obvious, and it is a bargain at $8 (in advance). Along with the grub, there is a rather extensive art show, live music at the plaza bandstand, and a vintage car show with more than one hundred participants, which covers both sides of the street for more than two blocks. Bring an appetite and water, wear a hat, and take it easy. Parking, well . . .

At sunset, there is a wonderful firework display at the Santa Fe Place mall on the south side of town. It is, of course, popular, but the wise can find a place to watch from nearby without getting caught in the traffic.

Along with the pyrotechnics, there are food trucks, live music, bounce houses, and lots of "ooohs" and "aaahs."

800-777-2489
santafe.org

SHOW
SOME LGBTQ PRIDE

Santa Fe has always been a place where the LGBTQ community feels welcome. So much so that *The Advocate*, one of the foremost publications focusing on LGBTQ lifestyle and politics, pointed out that "this is where seasoned gays come to center themselves, but not in a boring way."

We also offer a gay retirement center, Montecito, one of the few in the nation. Straight retirees are welcome there, as well.

Hence, Pride Week is huge in Santa Fe.

The Pride Parade seems to go on for miles and miles, is great fun, and also offers entertainment, music, and a popular opening ceremony. As of this year, Pride Week will include a birding adventure, a pool party, a "wear white" themed party, a women's dance, a tea dance with cocktails, a comedy show, and a sort of pop-up art show by Taz Morris, an award-winning artist.

And who knows what else will take place?

"Our streets are narrow, but our minds are not" kind of sums up what it is to be gay in Santa Fe.

Pride Santa Fe, 505-395-6243
pridesantafe.org

DITCH
THE CAR!

A popular bumper sticker in New Mexico reads, "My other car is in the arroyo." It is a tongue-in-cheek pronouncement on the illegal dumping that used to take place quite often in New Mexico.

But even if your car is in an arroyo or you don't want to rent one, there are other options besides walking, Lyft, or Uber in Santa Fe and the vicinity.

There are moped and e-bike rentals, pedicabs, and a city bus system, which doesn't always get the best reviews for its, umm, timeliness, but which is pretty reliable and inexpensive and covers the city quite well, every day.

And if you want to get out of town for a day and head to the "City Big," Albuquerque, try the Rail Runner, a tidy and sleek passenger train that goes to and fro from Belen, New Mexico. It is inexpensive and PDQ, as well.

2931 Rufina, 505-955-2001
santafenm.gov

TIP
Don't pretend to be a local, use your turn signal, although locals don't.

TIP

Don't ignore parking meters.
They operate Monday through Saturday until
6 p.m., although it seems that parking
enforcement isn't around much after 5 p.m. and
never on Sundays or federal holidays.

WEATHER OR NOT

The enlightened who know that New Mexico is a state and neither new nor Mexico might also know that our weather is an interesting subject. Although it can change at any given moment, there is always plenty of opportunity for outdoor activities, from snowboarding to day hikes.

There are several distinct areas in the state, with the south and southeast parts of the state being low desert, and the southwest being pure desert as part of the Chihuahuan Desert. And then there is the north.

The farther north one goes in New Mexico in the winter, the more one can expect a traditional "real" winter with snow and cold and bundling up. The farther south, much less.

Santa Fe does have four seasons, unlike Las Cruces, which has hot and not so hot. Here we have a real spring where things bloom and blossom, the weather turns milder, and the temperatures are friendly, but the wind often is not. Summer is often pleasant, although it can get into the nineties rather easily, with late summer seeing what is called the "monsoon" season, where brief but heavy rainstorms or thunderstorms often take place in the late afternoon.

Winter will see some snow, especially in the mountains, but unless it is a major storm it often melts in a day or so, thanks to *el sol*. Autumn, to me, is the best time of year. It can be colorful, often brilliantly so, as the aspen and cottonwood prepare to drop their leaves. The temperatures are pleasant, and there isn't much precipitation.

TIP

The highest recorded temperature occurred in 1994, when it hit 101 F; the lowest was in 2011, when it dipped to −18 F. And the nights are always cool . . . bring a sweater.

DAY TRIPPIN'
AT VALLES CALDERA AND JEMEZ SPRINGS

A beautiful, albeit narrow-winding road leads to these two unique places, which make for an interesting day trip from Santa Fe.

After passing through weird, homely, and secretive Los Alamos, about thirty minutes north of downtown Santa Fe, State Highway 4 first goes to Valles Caldera National Preserve, a mecca for hikers, wildlife watchers, people who live to fish, and in the winter cross-country skiers and snowshoe enthusiasts. It is an anomaly in New Mexico, a place with a lot of green and small lakes and ponds that are restful and peaceful, not to mention rarely visited. Please note that there are *no* services at the preserve.

Jemez Springs, a small, friendly village a bit farther up the road, hosts a wonderful hot springs park, where old and new bones can soak in comfort and serenity. You can also overnight at Jemez, which has a couple of cafés as well.

Take the backroad home past Jemez Springs and you can visit the amazing Jemez Pueblo and/or the nearby ghost town of Cabezon. You're welcome.

Valle Caldera, 39201 New Mexico Hwy. 4
575-829-4100, nps.gov/vall

Jemez Springs, State Hwy. 4
575-829-3540, jemezsprings.org

DISCOVER LITTLE-KNOWN NEW MEXICO HISTORY
AT PECOS PARK

Although this is not well known, New Mexico was the site for several battles during the Civil War.

In 1861, a small force of Confederate soldiers arrived in Mesilla, New Mexico, in the far south-central part of the state. Mesilla was made the capital of the new Confederate territory, and after several minor skirmishes in the area the Rebels headed north. They defeated a Union army at Fort Craig, in central New Mexico, captured Albuquerque and Santa Fe, and headed north, intent on capturing the booming Colorado goldfields, which were in high gear at the time. However, they were defeated in a major battle at Glorieta Pass, just north of Santa Fe.

The Pecos National Historical Park offers tours to provide more information on these events, along with a small museum. In addition, the park is home to the amazing Pecos ruin, which was once a mission and a pueblo for the local First Nations people.

This is also the place for one of the area's most beautiful Christmas-time events, when the ruins are lined with *farolitos* (a.k.a. luminaria—lanterns made of candles set in sand within paper bags) for one evening about a week before Christmas.

1 New Mexico Hwy. 63, Pecos, 505-757-7241, nps.gov/peco

NO SLEEPING
IN THESE TENTS!

One of the most beautiful and unusual day trips in the area will take you to the Cochiti Pueblo and to Tent Rocks, a formation of rocks that look like, well, pointy tents!

The Bureau of Land Management website notes, "The cone-shaped tent rock formations are the products of volcanic eruptions that occurred six to seven million years ago and left pumice, ash, and tuff deposits more than a thousand feet thick. Tremendous explosions from the Jemez volcanic field spewed pyroclasts (rock fragments), while searing hot gases blasted down slopes in an incandescent avalanche called a pyroclastic flow."

"Precariously perched on many of the tapering hoodoos are boulder caps that protect the softer pumice and tuff below. Some tents have lost their hard, resistant caprocks, and are disintegrating. While fairly uniform in shape, the tent rock formations vary in height from a few feet up to ninety feet."

The park is day-use only, and hiking is permitted only on three distinct and unique trails.

Kasha-Katuwe Tent Rocks National Monument, BLM Rd. 1011, County Rd. 22, 32. Cochiti Pueblo, 505-331-6259
blm.gov/visit/kktr

CLIMB
INTO CLIFF DWELLINGS
AT BANDELIER

One of New Mexico's truly amazing places is Bandelier National Monument. It is thought to have first been populated around 1150 AD, with a suggestion that the area had biped residents as far back as eleven thousand years ago.

Bandelier is home to numerous cliff dwellings, some of which are accessible to the public. The park provides easy access for the main trails and is day-use only. During the spring, summer, and fall, guests are shuttled via bus to the park, which covers nearly thirty-four thousand acres. It also has a great information center and small museum. All are run by the National Park Service.

There are also numerous petroglyphs, abundant wildlife, and often serene and quiet places for contemplation and centering.

15 Entrance Rd., Los Alamos, 505-672-3861
nps.gov/band

VIEW
ICONIC PETROGLYPHS
IN LA CIENEQUILLA

New Mexico is chock-full of petroglyphs, including an astounding site just minutes from the Santa Fe airport.

La Cienequilla, which translates to "little marsh," is a small park operated by the Bureau of Land Management; there is no fee, which makes it even more enticing.

The site contains a number of petroglyphs, which are thought to date from pre-contact (with Europeans) time. Many are thought to be from people who spoke the Keresan language and who are said to have lived around here between the thirteenth and seventeenth centuries.

The people who descended from the Keresan speakers may now be those who populate the Cochiti and Santo Domingo pueblos, just a bit south of Santa Fe. Favorite subjects for the rock art seem to be birds and a figure often called "Kokopelli," a flute player with a curved back.

674 Paseo Real, Highway 56, 575-758-8851
blm.gov/visit/la-cienequilla-petroglyphs

CRUISE THE BACK ROAD
TO MADRID

There is a beautiful back road coming into or leaving Santa Fe: State Highway 14, a National Scenic Byway that begins (or ends, your choice) in Santa Fe and winds its way through some beautiful scenery and groovy towns.

Leaving Santa Fe, Highway 14 takes you by the wayside communities of Lone Butte and San Marcos, just a short time before you get to the quaint and quiet village of Cerrillos (Little Hills). It is the home of a few interesting and little-known stops, such as Black Bird Saloon, a dive back into the "Old West"; the Casa Grande Trading Post; Cerrillos Turquoise Mining Museum and Petting Zoo; the Broken Saddle Riding Co.; and Cerrillos Hills State Park. A bit beyond Cerrillos is the ghost spot (not town) of Waldo, once home to a number of coke ovens. It is known as the Turquoise Trail.

The next stop must be Madrid (often pronounced "MAD-rid," sometimes "Mud-rid"), a town that was once completely for sale. Madrid had its own minor league baseball team during its high life and has now become a haven for artists, even though it has no water. Quaint and full of unique shops, along with the famed Mine Shaft Tavern, Madrid was once a booming coal mining town, now saved by art and mojo.

Turquoise Trail, State Hwy. 14
turquoisetrail.org

SHOPPING AND FASHION

"A PLACE IS NOT REALLY A PLACE WITHOUT A BOOKSTORE"

Sante Fe is a civilized place that still supports at least one independent bookstore; they seem to be as obsolete as carbon paper in many cities.

But Santa Fe's citizenry is well tended in this area, most especially by Collected Works, a good size book emporium.

Replete with a small coffee bar, run by local company Iconik Coffee Roaster, owner Dorothy Massey and her well-informed staff keep the place a hub of activity. They supply a good number of volumes, support local authors to the max and have numerous readings from local and nationally known authors and poets each month.

The store even offers a cozy space to curl up with a tome (perhaps one of my earlier works from a lesser publisher!) and a small outside patio where one can enjoy some very typical New Mexico blue sky while skimming a work from New Mexico author Anne Hillerman or a life on the Mexican border story by the late, great Charles Bowden.

The store has been in business for over 40 years and shows no signs of turning the page.

Quoting author Lailah Gifty Akita "The pleasure of reading is the greatest solitude."

202 Galisteo St, 505.988.4226
collectedworksbookstore.com

FIND
A NEW FAMILY MEMBER

Nope, not the two-legged kind, but rather the four-legged (or sometimes three-legged) kind.

The Santa Fe Animal Shelter and Humane Society is an official "no kill" shelter and is operated strictly with donations and grants. It does not use any tax money whatsoever.

The facility is a three-part operation, with one building housing admissions for found or unwanted pets. A full-service animal hospital is located in another building, and the third building houses adoptable critters and a small store.

The shelter has operated since 1939 and is housed in a state-of-the-art center on donated land, a tad west of Santa Fe. It also operates two retail stores that carry donated items such as clothing and small household furnishings, along with a spay-neuter clinic, which sometimes even offers free spay/neuter services and vaccinations to critters in need.

Utmost care is given to the "guests," no matter what the situation. And here is a testimonial—I am proud to say that I have worked there since 2014.

100 Caja del Rio, 505-983-4309
sfhumanesociety.org

KEEP
THAT CHRISTMAS SPIRIT GOING

Unless you live in Santa Claus, Indiana, or North Pole, Alaska, you probably won't find many cities with two Christmas decor stores that thrive year-round AND which are across the street from each other.

Susan Weber has operated Susan's Christmas Shop for over forty years now and shows no signs of slowing down. Besides scads of Christmas items, Weber also offers other seasonal goods for Valentine's Day and Easter.

The Shop—A Christmas Store, opened for business in 1977. It is owned by Rick and Janice Griego, who purchased the operation in 2002 from the originator, Edward Berry. The Shop—A Christmas Store opened for business in 1977. It is owned by Rick and Janice Griego, who purchased the operation in 2002 from the originator, Ed Berry. This store concentrates on Christmas, displaying about forty decorated trees that feature ornaments consisting mostly of Southwest designs conceived by various local artists.

SAY HEY, DOOD
AT DOODLET'S

Just in case the Five and Dime doesn't have the perfect souvenir of Santa Fe for you, Doodlet's should. If it doesn't, you are wa-a-a-ay too fussy.

Doodlet's is Santa Fe's answer to the old ads in the back of comic books that offered sea monkeys and x-ray specs for $1.

The store offers everything that you won't find elsewhere in our fair city, including 7,823 toys, 288 sugar skulls, and 347 types of candy. That doesn't include the nearly everything else that you've never seen before, all in one small shop.

The store opened in 1955 under the auspices of the unique and spontaneous personality of Theo Raven (actually Ruthling), and when Theo retired in 2010, she turned it over to her good friend Lisa Arnold.

If you miss this unique sundry store, you've missed the "real" Santa Fe.

120 Don Gaspar St., 505-983-3771
doodlets.com

TIP

Don't dress like a cowperson or a stylista. This will only ID you as a *tourista*, and besides that you'll probably look funny.

GET COSMIC, MAN!

During the 1980s and early '90s, "New Age" became a buzz term for alternative medicine, calming music, crystals, esoteric beliefs, and happenstance. The trend has somewhat dissipated over the years, but not in Santa Fe.

There are any number of unique and lesser-known practices in Santa Fe, including several folks who administer Reiki or read tarot. There are also several naturopaths, a number of herbalists, and about anything else New Age you can think of.

One of the best resources for all things alternative is the Ark, a bookstore that bills itself as a "metaphysical wonderland." It has been in business since about 1983 and always maintains a calming, peaceful atmosphere.

Barefoot Tarot is a new service, a kind of online clearinghouse for those seeking to know more about their inner workings. Tarot reader Miquella Mora offers guided meditation by appointment along with tarot and energy readings and something new called "Distance Reiki."

Santa Fe is a good place to get your inner gears cleansed!

The Ark, 133 Romero, 505-988-3709
arkbooks.com

Barefoot Tarot, 505-310-0383
facebook.com/barefoot.tarot.santafe

CELEBRATE OLD SCHOOL
AT RED RIVER MERCANTILE

Smaller, not inclined to feature designers, and website-free, Red River Mercantile is my personal store of choice in the city. Why? The store is "guy friendly," it is small, it is welcoming, and the offerings are unique and sturdy, which proves that a business can be successful without a website. In addition, owner Steve Traer has a great memory and offers terrific customer service.

The store has been open since 2011. Traer wanted a store that embraced the uniqueness of the city. In an interview he was quoted as saying, "Santa Fe is an amazing town. There's an ingrained ruggedness to this place that I want to explore through the merchandise that I sell in my shop. There's also a high level of sophistication that adds an interesting twist."

An online review of the store offered a great summary of those efforts: "If Ernest Hemingway, Joseph Conrad, and Cormac McCarthy needed duds they would come here!"

235 Don Gaspar, 505-992-1233

SHOP WITH CONFIDENCE
AT HARRY'S CLOTHING

Need a gift for the fashion-conscious gent or lady in your life? If so, Harry's can help you. Set in a welcoming boutique atmosphere, Harry's is another long-time business in Santa Fe, having opened in 1972 as Harry's Haberdashery.

Harry's tends to have mostly items for gents, with a small line of quality women's wear on the side. Harry's is often voted "best men's clothing store" in an annual poll of readers of the weekly *Santa Fe Reporter*, and you can count on finding the best of both worlds at this handsome shop.

And isnt afraid to trumpet itself: "Our store is also more than just a place to get a nice outfit; it's a place to be outfitted, completely. We carry good quality, brand-name products and we give good customer service that is knowledgeable and attentive at all times."

202 Galisteo, 505-988-1959
harrysclothing.com

FIND
EARTH-FRIENDLY GOODS
AT MAYA SANTA FE

An old-timer when it comes to independent stores in Santa Fe, Maya has been around for more than thirty years, dealing in products that are often a bit more earth- and socially-conscious than those at your usual store.

Part clothing store, part general store, it is a place for unique kitchen items, organic cotton clothing, and treats for the little snappers.

The clothing line tends to be lighter and airier than most, and many of the goods for the home are handmade by artisans from around the world.

108 Galisteo St., 505-989-7590
mayasantafe.com

TIP
Don't overdo the turquoise.
We've seen it all before.

BELIEVE IT:
"AND ALL YOUR FUTURE LIES BENEATH YOUR HAT"

In need of a new chapeau to cover your lovely locks? Guess what? You can find *real* hats here in Santa Fe, not just the generic off-the-shelf lids.

O'Farrell Hat Company custom makes the inventory: often cowperson hats, but it also does big hats, hybrid hats, crossover hats, Western dress hats, and distressed hats. And the staff don't care whether you are a gal or a guy.

It also has some cool hatbands, and it provides hatboxes for the few times in your life when you don't want a hat on.

Started by Kevin O'Farrell, who made hats for more than thirty years, the business is now in the hands of his son, Scott, who continues the family tradition.

111 E. San Francisco, 505-989-9666
ofarrellhatco.com

ESCAPE
THE BURNING RAYS
IN A MONTECRISTI CUSTOM HAT

It's always been a subject of deep discussion whether one should wear his/her cowperson hat at the dinner table when dining out. Of course one always should remove his hat in the presence of a lady, or tip it or touch the brim in acknowledgement of a person of the fair sex in passing. But take it off to eat? Iffy . . .

The solicitous staff at Montecristi Custom Hat Works can always help you find just the right hat to show off any or all of those etiquette skills (or one that will allow you to be a rude rube and keep it on). In business since 1978, proprietor Milton Johnson found his calling while visiting the small village of Montecristi, located on Ecuador's Pacific coast. It was here that he first espied the Montecristi Panama Hat, and the rest is history.

Montecristi's hats are at the high end of the price scale, but so is the quality. The store also carries hat bands (some made of real gold!), belts, and belt buckles.

And a final note of decorum concerning your new sombrero: If you ever see an old hat with the back side of the brim turned up, you'll know that the owner is not a cowperson. Those people have been a layin' their hats crown up when they take them off like the greenhorns they are.

322 McKenzie St., 505-983-9598
montecristihats.com

● ●

SUGGESTED
ITINERARIES

FILMOPHILES

Catch the Last Picture Show, 38

And Speaking of Movies . . . Attend Not One but Two Film Festivals, 34

Make Film History in Santa Fe!, 35

Appreciate Real Cinema, 32

THE ADVENTUROUS

Tour Santa Fe on Two Wheels, 61

Have an Authentic Western Adventure on Horseback, 65

Float through Life on a Raft!, 54

Get Your Outdoor Self On at Hyde Memorial State Park, 58

JUST FOR FUN

Eat, Drink, Sing at Cowgirl BBQ, 3

Go Soak Your Head in a Hot Spring Pool, 63

Be Entertained by New Mexico Politics, 46

Break Out the Peanuts and Cracker Jacks, 53

Learn to Read the Stars, 49

Discover the Crawling, the Flying, and the Creeping at Harrell House Bug Museum, 41

ART LOVERS' DELIGHT

Prepare to Be Awed by Spanish Colonial Folk Art, 90

Indulge in Hot Wax Art at the Museum of Encaustic Art, 74

Focus on International Art at the Ralph T. Coe Center, 96

Walk Among the Best Of Contemporary Native Arts, 94

Peruse Artifacts of Indian Arts and Culture, 88

Celebrate a New Mexico Art Icon, 97

HISTORIANS

Discover Little-Known New Mexico History at Pecos Park, 111

Look for Fact, not Fiction at the New Mexico
  Military Museum, 80

Something for Everyone at El Museo Cultural De Santa Fe, 95

Tour (One of) the Oldest Houses in the United States (?), 75

Climb Into Cliff Dwellings at Bandelier, 113

CHOWHOUNDS

Relax and Eat Well at Love Yourself Café, 6

Practice Your French at L'Olivier, 9

Experience Africa at the Jambo Café, 4

Meet and Greet Southwestern Style at Mucho Gusto, 20

Put on Your Bib at Harry's Roadhouse, 2

ACTIVITIES
BY SEASON

SPRING

Watch the Sunset from Cross of the Martyrs Park, 80

Tour Santa Fe on Two Wheels, 61

Add to Your Life List at the Randall Davey Audubon Center and Sanctuary, 82

Visit the Historic Walks of Santa Fe, 64

SUMMER

Break Out the Peanuts and Cracker Jacks, 53

Sponsor a New Artist at the Spanish Market, 102

Hike the Dale Ball Trails, 56

Shop and Socialize at Ye Olde Indian Market, 99

Float through Life on a Raft, 54

AUTUMN

Cruise the Back Road to Madrid, 115

Meditate on the Haiku Pathway, 47

Test Your Stamina at the Green Chile
Cheeseburger Smackdown, 101

While You're Already in the Neighborhood . . . Visit the Santa Fe
Botanical Garden, 92

WINTER

Ski Rugged Mountain Terrain, 52

Watch for Celebrities from Your Perch at the Teahouse, 26

Be Seen, but Not Heard at the Santa Fe Children's Museum, 72

Be Entertained by New Mexico Politics, 46

Get Your Outdoor Self on at Hyde Memorial State Park, 58

Go Soak Your Head in a Hot Spring Pool, 63

And Speaking of Movies . . . Attend not One but Two Film
Festivals, 34

INDEX

Acoma Pueblo, 75
AMP Concerts, 39
Ark, The, 126
Arroyo Chamisa Trail, 57
Astronomy Adventures, 49
Bandelier National Monument, 64, 113
Barefoot Tarot, 126
Battle of Bataan, 80
Battle of Santa Fe, 80
Blue Corn, 24
Bonanza Creek Ranch, 36
Broken Saddle Riding Co., 115
Buffalo Thunder, 48
Bumble Bee's Baja Grill, 8
Bureau of Land Management, 112, 114
Café Fina, 16
Casa Grande Trading Post, 115
Cathedral Basilica of St. Francis of Assissi, 68, 102
CCA, 32–33
Center for Contemporary Arts, 32
Cerrillos Hills State Park, 115
Cerrillos Turquoise Mining Museum, 115
Cerro Pelon Ranch, 81
Chihuahuan Desert, 108
Chili Line, 24
Cochiti Pueblo, 112
Collected Works Bookstore, 118

Cowgirl BBQ, 3, 135
Coyote Café, 60
Cross of the Martyrs Park, 84, 138
Dale Ball Trails, 56, 138
Doodlet's, 72, 124
Eaves Movie Ranch, 36
El Callejon, 60
El Camino Real, 76
El Museo Cultural de Santa Fe, 95, 136
El Rancho de las Golondrinas, 86
Encaustic Art Institute, 74
Food trucks, 2, 10, 24, 104
Garson Studios, 35
Georgia O'Keeffe Museum, 97
Geronimo, 18–19
Green Chile Cheesburger Smackdown, 101, 139
Green Tractor Farm, 12
Gruet Winery, 23
Haiku Pathway, 47, 139
Harrell House Bug Museum, 41, 135
Harry's Clothing, 128
Harry's Roadhouse, 2, 3, 136
Historic Walks of Santa Fe, 61, 64, 138
Honeymoon, 24
Hyde Memorial State Park, 58, 135, 139
Il Piatto Italian Farmhouse Kitchen, 12
Jambo Café, 4, 136
Japanese Internment Camp Remembrance Site, 70
Jean Cocteau Cinema, 32–33
Jemez Springs, 63, 110

KBAC 98.1, 42
Kokopelli Rafting Adventures, 54
L'Olivier, 9, 136
La Cienequilla, 114
La Plancha de Eldorado, 15
LGBTQ, 105
Loretto Chapel, 69
Love Yourself Café, 6, 136
Madrid, 115, 139
Maya, 130
Meow Wolf, 40
Montecristi Custom Hat Works, 133
Mucho Gusto, 20, 136
Museum Hill Bicycle Trail, 92
Museum of Contemporary Arts, 94
Museum of Encaustic Art, 74, 136
Museum of Indian Arts and Culture, 88
Museum of International Folk Art, 91
Museum of Spanish Colonial Art, 90, 102
National Scenic Byway, 115
New Mexico History Museum, 83
New Mexico Military Museum, 80, 136
O'Farrell Hat Company, 132
Palace of the Governors, 75, 83
Pantry, The, 14
Paper Dosa, 22
Pecos National Historical Park, 111
Petting Zoo, 115
Plaza, 9, 17, 58, 60, 68, 71, 76, 84, 92, 99, 102, 104
Poeh Cultural Center, 48

Rail Runner, 61, 106
Rail Trail, 57
Railyard Arts District, 44, 60, 95
Ralph T. Coe Center, 96, 136
Randall Davey Audubon Center and Sanctuary, 82, 138
Red River Mercantile, 127
Rotary Club of Santa Fe, 104
Roundhouse, 46
Route 66, 76–77
Rowley Farmhouse Ales, 24
Sabor Peruano, 7
San Miguel Church, 75
Santa Fe Animal Shelter and Humane Society, 120
Santa Fe Biking Tours, 61
Santa Fe Botanical Garden, 92–93, 139
Santa Fe Brewing, 24
Santa Fe Children's Museum, 5, 72, 139
Santa Fe Film Festival, 34
Santa Fe Food Depot, 103
Santa Fe Fuego, 53
Santa Fe Gallery Association, 44
Santa Fe Independent Film Festival, 34
Santa Fe Indian Market, 99
Sante Fe Margarita Trail, 28
Santa Fe National Cemetery, 70
Santa Fe Opera, 39, 45
Santa Fe Rafting, 54
Santa Fe River, 57
Santa Fe Studios, 35
Santa Fe Western Adventures, 65

Screen, The, 32–33
Second Street Brewery, 24, 60
Shop—A Christmas Store, The, 122–123
Ski Santa Fe, 52
Spanish Market, 90, 102, 138
Stargazer Portable Planetarium, 72
Sunrise Springs, 63
Susan's Christmas Shop, 122–123
Susan's Fine Wine and Spirits, 23
Sweetwater Harvest Kitchen, 5
Taos Pueblo, 36, 75
Teahouse, The, 26, 139
Ten Thousand Waves, 63
Tent Rocks, 112
Tia Sophia's, 17
Tumbleroot, 24
Tune-up Café, The, 13
Valles Caldera National Preserve, 110
Video Library, 38
Violet Crown Santa Fe, 33
Wander New Mexico, 60
West Circle Trail, 58
Wheelwright, The, 89
Wine and Chile Fiesta, 100
Zozobra, 98